MILITARY HISTORY OF THE IRISH CIVIL WAR

OTHER BOOKS IN THIS SERIES:

The Battle for Limerick city

The Summer Campaign in Kerry

The Battle for Kilmallock
(published September 2011)

The Battle for Cork
July–August 1922
(published September 2011)

THE FALL
OF DUBLIN

MILITARY HISTORY
OF THE IRISH CIVIL WAR

THE FALL
OF DUBLIN

28 JUNE TO 5 JULY 1922

LIZ GILLIS

SERIES EDITOR: GABRIEL DOHERTY

MERCIER PRESS
IRISH PUBLISHER – IRISH STORY

MERCIER PRESS
Cork
www.mercierpress.ie

© Text: Liz Gillis, 2011

© Foreword: Gabriel Doherty, 2011

ISBN: 978 1 85635 680 0

10 9 8 7 6 5 4 3 2 1

A CIP record for this title is available from the British Library

Printed and bound in the EU.

Dedicated to a true inspiration:
my late grandmother,
Betty Gillis

CONTENTS

ACKNOWLEDGEMENTS

This book would not have been written were it not for the support and help of so many wonderful people. I would like to thank Mary Feehan, Wendy Logue, Patrick Crowley and all the staff of Mercier Press. Thanks also to Eoin Purcell and Elaine Towns and the staff at UCD Archives and the National Library.

Special thanks to Niall Bergin, Anne-Marie Ryan and all my friends and colleagues at Kilmainham Gaol Museum, your help and support have been amazing throughout. A special mention to all the staff at Military Archives: Commandant Victor Laing, Captain Stephen MacEoin, Private Adrian Short, Alan Manning, Chris Donovan, Lisa, Noelle and Hugh, I cannot thank you enough for all your help over the years.

When writing this book I was so fortunate to meet so many people whose relatives had fought in Dublin: Kathleen Manley-Walton, Michael Manley, Sheila Manley-Maguire, Kathleen Cregan-Quadrato, Mike Connolly, Frank Murphy and family, Jack Murphy, Derek Jones, Austin Bolger, Antonette McSweeney, Shelia Murray, Margaret O'Byrne, Eamon Fitzpatrick and Danny Fitzpatrick, and Liam Doyle; thank you all for sharing your stories.

Many thanks to Paddy Kelly, who was so generous in sharing his father's collection of documents and photographs from the period and for granting permission to use them. I would also like to thank Rory and Peadar Breslin and family for granting permission to use family photographs. Thanks also to Mick Meehan, Ernie Waters, Shay Courtney, Patrick Cafferty and Terry Fagan.

I am indebted to Cormac O'Malley for granting me full access to his father Ernie O'Malley's notebooks and for taking the time to answer all my queries about them. To Las Fallon, I cannot express my gratitude enough; thanks to you so many men who were forgotten for so long are now being remembered. My heartfelt thanks to Cathal Brugha, who was so forthcoming with information and was more than generous in sharing his family history with me. I would also like to thank Francis E. Maguire for granting me permission to quote extracts from his father John A. Pinkman's diaries.

I would like to give a special mention to Mícheál Ó Doibhilín: thank you for not only drawing the maps, but also for just being you; Paul O'Brien, who was responsible for getting the book off the ground; Peter McMahon, Ciarán Barry, Emma King, Shane Kenna, Catherine Murphy, Diane O'Reilly, Derek Horan, Tom Caulfield, Susan Doyle, Derek O'Callaghan, Martin O'Dwyer (Bob) and Pádraig Óg Ó Ruairc; you all played a part in making this book come together and I am forever grateful for your help and support.

To my family, who have always been there to support everything I have done, I cannot express in words my thanks. My brothers John and Pat, my nephew Mikey and niece Pheobe, my brother-in-law Gerry, Lydia, Jack and Aunt May, and my extended family, Mary Crowe, Brendan, Rachel, Mary, Pat, Gerry, Nicole and Neil, thank you all for your encouragement. To my Uncle Pat, you have done more for me than you realise and I am forever grateful to you for all your support over the years. To my older sister Mimi, I cannot thank you enough, you have been more than a sister to me and you will never know just how much you mean to me.

And to my fiancé, James, whose love and encouragement has been constant throughout everything I have done. Without it I could not have written this book.

Finally I would like to thank my dad Mick. You have made every wish and dream I had a reality, you are the best father, my best friend and above all you are my hero, and none of this would have been possible without you.

FOREWORD

Given their importance in the histories of those nations unlucky enough to have endured them, it is surprising to note that the first shots of many civil wars have been fired in peripheral locales, bereft of obvious political, economic or strategic significance. To take the most significant example in the modern era, Fort Sumter, a miniscule installation at the mouth of Charlestown harbour, was a far from prepossessing location for the start of the most devastating conflict in American history, and a similar provincial pattern was evident in the origins of many internecine conflicts in twentieth-century Europe, in countries as disparate as Finland in 1918, Spain in 1936 and Bosnia in 1992.

The Irish Civil War was fundamentally different in this respect, in that its opening salvoes were fired from positions in the very centre of the capital city, Dublin; these shots were fired moreover, in the certain knowledge that the attack on the anti-Treaty garrison in the Four Courts would immediately result in general, nationwide warfare. The Irish Civil War, of course, differs in other respects from the conflicts mentioned above, not least in its limited scale, but most significantly in the fact that the initial, and swiftly-concluded, exchanges proved to be the decisive engagement of the entire campaign. Within a matter of days the strategic heart of the new state was completely, and rather unexpectedly, in the hands of pro-Treaty troops, who capitalised on this initial victory with a seemingly irresistible advance southwards and westwards, slowing down only, and temporarily, when they hit their enemy's Munster heartlands. In registering this stunning strategic victory Michael Collins further enhanced his burgeoning reputation as a political and military figure of substance – but, just perhaps, in so doing he also sowed, in his hour of victory, the seeds of hubris that were to lead to his own death in the by-ways of west Cork a few weeks later.

The narrative of these crucial, formative days in the history of modern Ireland, forms the basis for Liz Gillis' study. It is a drama with many characters (heroic or villainous depending on one's viewpoint), sub-plots, unexpected twists and, above all, a brutally swift denouement. It is adroitly delivered here, with the benefit of source materials unavailable to the surprisingly small number of authors who have written on the topic in the past. Her exploration of the ideological, personal and political backdrop to the bombardment of the Four Courts, and the subsequent collapse of the anti-Treaty forces in the capital, repay detailed consideration, as does her plaintive closing rhetorical question as to the purpose of it all. All told, it is an exemplary volume in Mercier's *Military History of the Irish Civil War* series.

Without wishing to go too far beyond the military focus of the series, I will close by seeking to posit the first act of this national tragedy in a slightly broader context. Given the limited loss of life and relatively small scale of the material destruction experienced during the eleven months of fighting, the explanation as to why the legacy of the Irish Civil War is so much more enduring than that of more destructive conflicts in other lands must surely be sought as much, if not more, in the realm of collective social psychology as in the details of its military events, narrowly defined. There are many aspects to this key element of national *mentalité*, with the obvious ones being the contempt of the pro-Treaty side for their opponents' apparent indifference to the democratic decision of the Dáil in January 1922, and the disgust of the anti-Treatyites at their former comrades' perceived abandonment of the republic. In the context of the current volume, however, the crux surely lies in the fact that this landmark battle, fought in the heart of the nation's capital, and for the soul of its people, in the very streets that six years before had witnessed the sacred days of the Easter Rising, produced a complete, and almost bloodless, victory for the pro-Treaty side, and a republican collapse from entrenched positions in a fashion the British had never been able to effect. The resulting sense of shame and demoralisation, and the inevitable search for scapegoats on the losing side, was matched only by the barely-contained contempt harboured by the victors for their erstwhile comrades. Had the fighting lasted longer, had the victory been closer, had the casualties been greater in this initial phase, perhaps the bitterness engendered by the outcome, paradoxically, might – just might – have been less keenly etched on the national psyche in the long run. As with all counter-factual history we can, of course, never have clear answers to such questions, but, at minimum, we can certainly thank Liz Gillis for giving us the solid ground upon which such informed speculation can rest.

Chapter 1

The Treaty to the Split

On 11 July 1921, the people of Ireland woke to the news that hostilities between the Irish Republican Army (IRA) and British forces had officially ended. The War of Independence was at last over and, unsurprisingly, the ordinary citizens who had suffered greatly over the preceding two and a half years had something to hope for – peace. No one knew what the future would hold for the country, but at that time the joy and elation felt throughout Ireland was immeasurable. This state of affairs was to be short-lived, however, when less than one year later, two armies would again bear arms in Ireland. This time it would be Irishman killing Irishman, and the first shots of what was to become the Irish Civil War were heard on 28 June 1922, when the battle for Dublin city began.

The signing of the Anglo-Irish Treaty on 6 December 1921 ended the possibility of Ireland becoming a united thirty-two-county Republic, and with it ended the unity of the Republican movement that had prevailed in previous years. For some, the Treaty was the best that could be achieved at that time; to use Michael Collins' words, it was 'a stepping-stone' to getting full independence later. For many, however, it was seen as a betrayal of the Republican ideal and an insult to all of those who had suffered and died for the Republic. However, under the threat from Britain of 'immediate and terrible war', five Irishmen signed the Treaty in the early hours of 6 December. It was a document that gave so much hope yet would cause so much tragedy, which would be felt in Ireland for years to come.[1]

The Treaty split both Sinn Féin, the political wing of the Republican movement, and the IRA, the military wing. Between the signing of the document on 6 December 1921 and 7 January 1922, there was much debate in the Dáil on the merits of accepting or rejecting the Treaty. Both the pro-Treaty side, headed by Michael Collins and Arthur Griffith, and the anti-Treaty side, under the leadership of Éamon de Valera and Cathal Brugha, in often highly charged discussions, sought to obtain a result that would appeal to both sides of the divide. This, however, proved to be an unrealistic goal, though at that time no one believed it to be so.

On 7 January 1922, the Dáil ratified the Treaty by sixty-four votes to fifty-seven. De Valera and his supporters left the Dáil in protest. With them went the hope that the Republican movement could survive intact, but even at this stage the idea that civil war might actually break out was far from people's minds. Despite the politicians making their decision, the army still believed that an all-out split could be avoided. For the next six months it was the army and not the politicians who really tried to find a solution, but in the end it proved to be a futile effort.

On 9 January 1922, Arthur Griffith replaced Éamon de Valera as president of the Dáil. Richard Mulcahy replaced

Cathal Brugha as Minister for Defence, after which he stated that 'the Army [IRA] will remain the Army of the Irish Republic'.[2] However, the army was split on the issue of the Treaty: most of the General Headquarters staff (GHQ) accepted it, but the majority of the pre-Truce IRA rejected the Treaty.[3] This sentiment was made known to Mulcahy in a letter from the anti-Treaty IRA on 11 January, requesting the holding of an Army Convention to discuss whether the IRA would revert to its independent position before it came under the control of the Dáil. The army would reaffirm its allegiance to the Republic and would remain the army of the Republic. An Executive would be appointed which would control the army, and they would draw up a constitution that would be submitted to another convention. If this was refused, an independent headquarters staff would be set up.[4] This proposal was not supported by many on the anti-Treaty side, including Cathal Brugha. He strongly believed, as did Mulcahy, that the army should, and must, remain under the control of the Dáil.

On 14 January 1922, the Provisional Government was established, with Michael Collins as chairman. The Dáil had not yet been dissolved and continued to function as normal. It was decided that an election on the Treaty would be held within six months and in that time a new constitution would be drawn up. On 16 January, Dublin Castle was formally handed over by the British to the new government. It was quickly realised that the Provisional Government needed an army that would be loyal to it, as it could not depend on the support of the IRA. On 18 January, Richard Mulcahy and Michael Collins met with the anti-Treaty officers to assess the situation. While not dismissing the idea of a convention being held, Mulcahy made it very clear that the army was subject to the control of the Dáil, the elected government, and could not remove itself from such control. The anti-Treaty officers felt that they would have no say in the setting up of the new army and that the Republic would be betrayed. A compromise was reached with great difficulty. The proposed convention would be postponed until March, and in the meantime a committee, consisting of members from each side, would be set up to ensure that GHQ would not undermine or subvert the Republic.

This suggestion was not satisfactory to the majority of the Republican officers, who wanted to set up a headquarters that would be independent of GHQ. However, Liam Lynch, O/C 1st Southern Division, the largest and strongest division of all, was reluctant at this time for an independent headquarters to be established as it could lead to conflict, and after much deliberation Mulcahy's offer was accepted. Even though the majority followed Lynch, Ernie O'Malley, O/C 2nd Southern Division, broke away from the control of GHQ.

It seemed as though an all-out split was inevitable, but it was still believed at this time that civil war could be avoided. Men such as Cathal Brugha and Liam Lynch, seen as the extremists on the Republican side by many in subsequent years, did everything they could to prevent civil war from breaking out. On the pro-Treaty side were Michael Collins and Richard Mulcahy, who also sought a way to avoid a war that could damage the country for generations. By delaying the convention, Mulcahy hoped that the Free State Constitution would be drawn up and then, and only then, when the constitution was put before everyone, would the army decide on what action to take.[5]

On 31 January 1922, Beggars Bush Barracks was taken over by members of the 'Dublin Guard', in total fewer than fifty men, under the command of Brigadier-General Paddy O'Daly.[6] Beggars Bush was to be the headquarters of what soon became the pro-Treaty National Army. After this, other barracks were handed over by the British to the IRA, regardless of the men's loyalty to the Treaty. Dublin was the exception; no barracks in the Dublin area were handed over to the anti-Treaty IRA. The Provisional Government was now in a precarious position and its army numerically weak. More importantly, it was even weaker in terms of experienced men as most of the pre-Truce IRA were anti-Treaty. However, little was done by the anti-Treaty IRA to seize the initiative at this point. This reluctance to act would cost the Republicans dearly later.

By mid-February, with the British evacuation well under way, recruitment for the new National Army began.[7] There were many problems with organisation, and even with the supply of uniforms and arms, but a new army slowly began to emerge.[8]

At the end of February, tension between the two sides of the army increased when events in Limerick threatened to lead to conflict. Limerick was a key position for both the Republicans and the pro-Treaty forces, and both wanted to take over the barracks being evacuated. After much discussion, it was eventually agreed that the Republicans would remain in two barracks, while Limerick Corporation would hold the police barracks. The pro-Treaty forces would have to leave.[9] This compromise did not reflect well on the Provisional Government and Arthur Griffith was most vocal in his opposition to it. He believed that civil war was unavoidable, and the sooner the government acted, the sooner the war would be over.

On 15 March, as a result of the Limerick crisis, the proposed Army Convention was prohibited by the government, which stated that any officer who attended the convention would be suspended from the army. The anti-Treaty IRA disregarded the ban and it was decided that the convention would be held on 26 March.

In the meantime the anti-Treaty IRA decided that a new General Headquarters staff should be established, and Liam Lynch was elected chief-of-staff. Liam Mellows was elected quartermaster general; Rory O'Connor, director of engineering; Seamus O'Donovan, director of chemicals; Seán Russell, director of munitions; Ernie O'Malley, director of organisation; and Joe Griffin, director of intelligence. These appointments were temporary until the convention could be held with an election to appoint permanent positions. In the meantime, they set up a temporary headquarters in the Gaelic League Hall at 44 Parnell Square.

On 26 March, the proclaimed convention was held in the Mansion House, Dublin. More than 200 delegates, representing fifty-two out of the seventy-three IRA brigades, attended.[10] The outcome of the convention was that:

> The Delegates reaffirmed their allegiance to the Republic, denounced the Treaty, and elected an Executive of 16 in whom they vested supreme control of the army. The Executive repudiated the authority of the Minister for Defence [Mulcahy], and the

Chief of Staff [Eoin O'Duffy] and most significantly, repudiated the authority of Dáil Éireann.[11]

It was also proposed that a new Army Constitution be drawn up by the Executive (of which Liam Lynch was elected chief-of-staff), and that the Belfast Boycott be reintroduced.[12] It was also decided that a second Army Convention would be held to draft the constitution and elect a permanent Executive.

Lynch and his men set up headquarters in Barry's Hotel, in Gardiner's Row. Annie Farrington, who had only purchased the hotel a few weeks before the convention, remembers the men who stayed there:

> We had a dreadful crowd of guests for that occasion, a lot of them from Galway and the West. There was terrific excitement. There was great diversity of views and they were arguing it out. They never came to blows … The discussions were very heated but I had no time to listen to them as we were so busy trying to keep the meals and the beds going and we did not yet know our way about too well.[13]

Of the men who stayed in the hotel, she states:

> Among the visitors I especially remember Liam Lynch, Moss Twomey, Dick [Richard] Barrett and Joe McKelvey from Belfast … Liam Lynch was a marvellous character and the other lads used to warn us not to say anything flippant before him, as he was very religious and they looked upon him as a saint … Barrett was a very nice boy too and had a good sense of humour. He was a delicate sort of lad … They were lovely people to have in the house, they were so well-behaved.[14]

Meanwhile, on 28 March, a statement issued by the Executive demanded that recruitment to both the National Army and the newly formed Civic Guard should cease.

The second Army Convention was held on 9 April at the Mansion House. The new Republican Constitution was ratified: the army would retain the title of the Irish Republican Army and would continue to function as had the pre-Truce IRA; that is, it would be on a volunteer basis. Its aims were to uphold the independence of the Republic, to protect the rights of its citizens and to serve an established Republican government that was wholly loyal to the Republic and its people.

It was decided that this army would be controlled by an Executive of sixteen, who would appoint an Army Council of seven members and the chief-of-staff of the army. A headquarters staff was also elected.[15] Since the anti-Treaty IRA were now cut off from financial assistance from the Provisional Government, it was decided that banks all over the country were to be raided to finance them: 'receipts in the names of the officers in charge of raids were to be given for all monies received'.[16]

A motion was put forward that the forthcoming election be proclaimed. This was opposed by many of the Republicans, including Cathal Brugha, Tom Hales, Liam Lynch, Florrie O'Donoghue and Seán O'Hegarty. The latter four were members of the Executive; all five believed that it was the right of the people to at least have the chance to decide whether they accepted or rejected the Treaty, and as they had been elected by the people, they had to honour that right. This motion was defeated, but divisions in the anti-Treaty side were beginning to show.

On 13 April, Liam Mellows issued an ultimatum to the Dáil that the army should reunite:

> He demanded that the existing Republic be maintained under a Republican Dáil government, that the IRA be controlled by an independent executive, that the IRA be financed by the Dáil, that the policing of the country be carried out by the IRA and the civic guard be disbanded, and that no elections take place on the Treaty while the threat of war with England exists.[17]

CHAPTER 2

TAKEOVER OF
THE FOUR COURTS

In the early hours of Good Friday, 14 April, the newly elected anti-Treaty IRA Executive issued orders for the Dublin Brigade to seize the Four Courts.[1] Shortly after midnight, members of the Executive, including Liam Mellows and Ernie O'Malley, together with members of the Dublin Brigade, proceeded to the courts.

The seizure of such a building was a huge and purely symbolic act, as it 'dramatised the failure of the Provisional Government's authority'.[2] However, the reality of the situation was that the Executive had realised they needed a more suitable headquarters. It was not their intention to be there for a substantial amount of time because they still believed that civil war could be averted. In an interview with the press soon after the takeover, Rory O'Connor stated that:

The occupation of the building should not be taken in any way as a coup d'etat, nor did it indicate the beginning of a revolution. 'There is going to be no revolution,' he added ... He said they wanted that place [the Four Courts] as the premises they had in Parnell Sq. were not sufficient to accommodate them ... It was their intention to immediately remove their headquarters from Parnell Sq. to the Four Courts, where a publicity office, amongst other things, would be set up.[3]

In all, about 120 men took over the courts. Describing the take-over, Ernie O'Malley wrote:

> As we approached the Courts, the heavy massive buildings took blurred shapes in the darkness. The dome could be seen faintly against the sky. We leaned against the parapet opposite to the main gate. We approached the main gate. Some stooped down and gave the others a back. They climbed over the railings and disappeared in the dark.[4]

Men from Tipperary under the command of Seamus Robinson, O/C 3rd Tipperary Brigade, reinforced the garrison.

The Four Courts Hotel, next to the courts in Morgan's Place, was also taken over and preparations were made to barricade it, but the hotel was soon evacuated and the garrison joined their comrades in the Four Courts. A headquarters block was established at the rear of the complex, facing the Bridewell Prison, and the barricading of the courts began. Whatever was at hand was used to fortify the building, including barbed wire and sandbags. Many windows were barricaded with 'heavy legal tomes, law books and weighty ledgers, and tin boxes filled with earth'.[5] The men were grouped into six sections and allotted to various posts throughout the complex. Paddy O'Brien, 4th Battalion, Dublin Brigade, veteran of the War of Independence, was appointed O/C of the Four Courts garrison. He was, according to O'Malley, 'above medium height, straight, soldierly ... Blue-eyed, serious, good featured, tireless in energy.'[6] O'Brien in turn appointed Seán Lemass, 1st Battalion, Dublin Brigade, a veteran of both the Easter Rising and the War of Independence, as his adjutant.

It soon became apparent that the garrison would need an ample supply of weapons if and when the fight did come. To enable them to make mines and grenades, a suitable building had to be found. The records office was chosen, as it was the most isolated building in the complex. The orderlies section (also known as No. 5 section), most of whom had been members of Na Fianna, were in charge of guarding this building. Leo Henderson, 2nd Battalion, Dublin Brigade, was appointed director of the Belfast Boycott and had offices in the ground floor of the Four Courts.

The Four Courts was a vast complex to hold and fortify adequately. The Tipperary garrison soon left the courts to return to their own area, leaving approximately 180 men of the 1st and 2nd Battalions of the Dublin Brigade to defend the building. Ideally, at least 300 men would be required to mount a proper defence of the building. As it was, Paddy O'Brien had to defend the building as best he could with the number of men he had at his disposal. Together with Ernie O'Malley and Oscar Traynor, O/C Dublin Brigade, the men worked out a plan of action should the pro-Treaty forces decide to attack the courts. The Republican forces would have snipers in the area surrounding the Four Courts, with some houses being taken over for that purpose. Similarly, the army barracks in the city would be isolated using this method. Bridges were to be blown up and streets barricaded to impede troop movement. Troops surrounding the courts would themselves be encircled and attacked. However, the Army Executive, stationed in the courts, refused to allow the plans to be put into action, as this would be seen as an offensive move by the Republicans, and they intended not to be the ones to fire the first shot.

This reluctance by some members of the Executive to act in a proactive way was fatal. It also completely undermined Paddy O'Brien's position as commandant of the garrison. This was to be the first of many similar decisions to be taken by the Executive.

Although the takeover of the Four Courts emphasised the split in the IRA, there was still hope that armed conflict could be avoided. Over the next two and a half months a nervous tension existed between the opposing sides; only time would tell if they would be able to resolve their differences peacefully.

CHAPTER 3

APRIL TO JUNE 1922

While the takeover of the Four Courts by the Republicans was a direct and open challenge to the Provisional Government, they were at this time in no real position to act against them. Although the government was building up a National Army, recruitment was limited and equipment in short supply. John A. Pinkman, who joined the army in early March, wrote:

> Anyone wishing to join the National Army had to have served in the Volunteers and upon joining was, in fact, transferred from the IRA into the National Army ... open recruitment for the National Army did not begin until after the Civil War had broken out ... My first impression of Beggar's Bush barracks was that almost everything about it appeared lackadaisical. None of the recently recruited soldiers, including myself, was provided with a uniform. In fact only a mere handful of soldiers in the barracks were fully uniformed; many of the rest were dressed partly in uniform and partly in civilian clothes.[1]

Also at this time, the government could not depend on total loyalty from the members of the army. Resignations and desertions were commonplace, as many men decided that they were either on the wrong side or that they had no stomach to actually take up arms against their former comrades. Hughie Early, 4th Battalion, Dublin Brigade IRA, who had enlisted in the National Army early on, left because he failed, after three weeks, to gain an army commission. Denis Fitzpatrick, 1st Battalion, Dublin Brigade, who had seen active service in both the Easter Rising and the War of Independence, decided that his loyalties lay with the Republicans. Both men joined their comrades in the Four Courts.

Many were given the choice of walking away from the army if they genuinely felt they could not support the Treaty. According to Pinkman, Paddy O'Daly, O/C Dublin Guards, addressed his men:

> He assured us that no animosity would be shown against anyone who stepped forward ... He also promised that no action would subsequently be taken against those who left the army ... All he asked for ... was that those who wished to leave should hand in to stores their uniforms, rifles, ammunition, and their other military gear before they left.[2]

By this time, the Provisional Government had received from the British Government '4,000 rifles, 2,200 revolvers, and six machine guns, together with corresponding amounts of ammunition'.[3] A number of armoured cars had also been left by the British on evacuation. The government were, however, reluctant to act, as the Republicans outnumbered them in terms of men, and as a result of the raid on the British Admiralty ship *Upnor* at Cork in March, they were relatively well armed. In that raid, members of the 1st Southern Division, under the command of Seán O'Hegarty, were successful in capturing the ship's cargo of arms. The arms were landed at Ballycotton and removed successfully by lorry. Michael Collins felt that the British allowed the raid to happen, to undermine the authority of the Provisional Government, a claim the British denied. In the raid, the Republicans seized roughly:

> 1,500 rifles, 55 Lewis guns, 6 Maxim guns, 3 Vickers guns and 500,000 rounds of ammunition (.303), as well as 1,000 each of revolvers and .455 automatic pistols with a comparable amount of ammunition, 3000 hand grenades and a quantity of rifle grenade throwers.[4]

Paddy O'Connor of the Dublin Guards best summed up the reality that the Provisional Government faced at this time:

> We numbered 800 all ranks, the Second Eastern division was 500. With the 200 from Kilkenny, it was reckoned we would have 1,000 men available in Dublin. To oppose this force the irregulars had in Dublin an estimated force of 3,000 men, and there was in the country a force of 20,000–30,000 men. It was hardly likely that their HQ staff would remain in the Four Courts to be bottled up nor was it likely that they would allow us to defeat their Dublin force, and gain undisputed control of the city.[5]

Meanwhile, the British, unnerved by what was happening, stopped the evacuation of their troops.

Back at the courts, the garrison by now had in their possession an armoured car, which they named 'The Mutineer'. Ernie O'Malley had been sent from the courts to inspect Republican positions, mainly in the west of Ireland. On his way back to Dublin he visited Templemore Barracks in County Tipperary, whose garrison had recently declared their loyalty to the Republican side. The pro-Treaty forces had sent down a patrol of troops in an armoured car as a threat to the mutineers. As a result of this act, Brigadier Leahy, O/C of the garrison, ordered his men to capture the armoured car. O'Malley realised what a huge asset the car would be to the men in the courts, and in exchange for the car Leahy was given arms. The car was then brought to Dublin. Describing it, O'Malley wrote:

> It was covered with heavy plates of bullet-proof steel. The engine was long, a Rolls Royce. On top was a revolving steel turret which contained a Vickers gun, capable of long sustained fire without overheating; the ammunition was in strips, side by side in narrow belts. Near the driving wheel was a long steel rod with a handle projecting into the car; the rod opened or shut the steel flaps protecting the front radiator: the engine would overheat if the flaps were not opened occasionally. There were small loop-holes which could be closed with small steel shutters; they were for the revolvers of the crew.[6]

Though hostilities appeared to be imminent, serious efforts were still being made by both sides to stop the inevitable from happening.

On 1 May, the army officers' statement was published; the document was signed by officers from both sides of the divide, and they suggested that, in order to unify the army, the Treaty should be accepted and a non-contested election be held, after which a coalition government would be set up.[7] The anti-Treaty Army Executive immediately denounced this; however, it did provide the impetus needed for the politicians to try again to find a way to work together. A Dáil Peace Committee was set up, headed by Kathleen Clarke, widow of Tom Clarke, who was executed for his part in the Easter Rising; though their efforts were noble, no progress was made and less than three weeks later talks between the two sides ceased.[8]

Because of the army officers' statement, a Joint Army Committee was established on 4 May, consisting of members from both sides of the IRA.[9] In an effort to preserve unity, a truce was declared in order to put an end to the sporadic outbreaks of violence that had been taking place between the pro- and anti-Treaty forces. The truce was later extended. Although ultimately they could not agree, one thing that did act as a basis for unity was the situation in Northern Ireland.

Frank Aiken, O/C of the 4th Northern Division, which was at this time neutral, appealed to both sides not to forget the Catholic population in the six counties who, as a result of escalating violence being carried out against them, were being forced to leave their homes and flee south for safety. For months, members of the loyalist community, with the backing of the Special Constabulary, had targeted the Catholic population, resulting in many deaths. In response, the Northern IRA did what they could to destabilise the northern state, which resulted in even more reprisals against the Catholic population. This renewed interest in the northern campaign helps to explain why the anti-Treaty IRA were not forced to leave the Four Courts. According to Rory O'Connor, 'Someone suggested the evacuation of the Four Courts, and Richard [Mulcahy] laughingly said that as long as we held that place, the war against NE Ulster would be attributed to us. We, of course, had no objection.'[10]

As a result of the efforts being made by the army, Michael Collins and Éamon de Valera entered into discussions which culminated in the signing of the Collins-de Valera Pact on 20 May. Under the terms of the pact, it was agreed that a coalition panel of pro- and anti-Treaty Sinn Féin candidates would be put before the people. Rather than voting on whether to accept or reject the Treaty, the people would instead be voting on who they preferred to see elected to the government. A coalition executive was to be established, including a Minister for Defence representing the army, along with nine other ministers from both sides: five ministers from the majority party and four from the minority. If this coalition broke down, then a general election was to be held in which the people would decide whether to accept the Treaty or not. There was no reference to the Treaty in the pact.[11]

Not only was this unacceptable to the British, it was also unacceptable to many members of the Dáil including, surprisingly, Cathal Brugha. He was adamant that the people be given the chance to vote for a Free State or a Republic. Brugha's suggestion that the people should decide on the issue was rejected, after which he made a most impassioned and prophetic speech in which he said:

> I for one would prefer to die by an English bullet or an Orange bullet rather than by a bullet fired by one of the men with whom we have been fighting together during the last six years ... I am never going to fire a bullet at any of these men and I hope that I am not going to die by a bullet from any of them.[12]

In light of the pact, there seemed to be a real chance for the military to avoid civil war. An Army Council had also been set up to secure unity in the army, consisting of four officers from each side.[13] They would decide between themselves who would take the role of Minister for Defence and other army positions. Talks between the two sides continued and on 26 May the Four Courts Executive agreed to evacuate key buildings in the city, with the exception of the Four Courts and those being used to house the Belfast refugees. They also agreed to stop commandeering cars and private property, and property already in their possession was to be returned.

Throughout June both sides worked together on the northern offensive. Arms were readily given to the Republicans by the pro-Treaty forces. In return, the Republicans sent their guns to the northern IRA divisions so that no trace of pro-Treaty involvement would be discovered by the British.

On 14 June, the proposals agreed by the Army Council were put before the anti-Treaty Executive. The proposed coalition GHQ staff was unacceptable to the majority of the Executive, who felt that the positions allotted on the council were not in their favour, and thus it was rejected.

Finally, on 16 June, the people had their chance to vote. A few days before the election, Collins repudiated the pact, urging the people to vote for whom they thought would best represent them. In reality, it was highly unlikely that the pact would have worked. The Free State Constitution, on which the hopes of the Republicans, especially Liam Lynch, depended, was published on the morning of the election. It stated, among other things, that the Provisional Government would appoint the governor general and that all men and women over the age of twenty-one could vote; however, *every* member of the Dáil must swear an oath of allegiance to the crown. No Republican would do this, so the idea of a coalition government was dead in the water.

Pro-Treaty Sinn Féin won fifty-eight seats, and anti-Treaty Sinn Féin won thirty-six. Non-Sinn Féin candidates who were pro-Treaty won thirty-four seats in total.[14] The people had spoken. There was nothing left for the Provisional Government to do but to act against the Republicans. The British were most eager to see this happen; however, they would have to wait a little longer for their hopes to become a reality.

CHAPTER 4

18–26 JUNE

On 18 June, the third Army Convention was held in the Mansion House. Liam Lynch tried to put the proposals on army unity before the delegates, despite them having been rejected by the Executive, as he felt that the delegates should be given a chance to decide whether they wanted to accept the proposals and thus avert civil war. Before he was able to do this, however, Tom Barry, a member of the Executive since 12 June, put forward his resolution that unless the British troops left Dublin within seventy-two hours, hostilities would be resumed against them. This, Barry believed, could unite the army. The motion was put to a vote and passed. However, the result was challenged because a brigade was present that had not been represented at the previous convention, and on a second count of the votes the motion was narrowly defeated by 118 votes to 103, after which the defeated delegates, including most of the Executive, left the convention and went to the Four Courts. Liam Lynch was deposed as chief-of-staff and replaced by Joe McKelvey, formerly O/C Belfast Brigade, who had been appointed assistant chief-of-staff after the Treaty was signed and the IRA initially split. Liam Lynch and his supporters from the 1st Southern Division, including Liam Deasy and

Seán Moylan, went to the Clarence Hotel and set up headquarters there. Out of the sixteen-man Executive, twelve were in the Four Courts.

The next day, Lynch and his men tried to gain entry to the Four Courts, but found themselves locked out. As Todd Andrews commented: 'The Four Courts garrison had amputated their most powerful limb, effectively isolating themselves in the last bastion of the Republic.'[1] This split in the anti-Treaty ranks offered a lifeline to the Provisional Government. If Lynch and his men could be kept out of the fray, it might be possible for the pro-Treaty forces to act quickly and isolate the Four Courts garrison.

On 22 June, Sir Henry Wilson, military advisor to the Northern Ireland Government, was shot dead outside his home in Eaton Square, London, by two members of the London IRA: Reginald Dunne and Joseph O'Sullivan.[2] The Four Courts garrison were blamed for the shooting, and as a result of Wilson's death the British government put immense pressure on the Provisional Government to assert its authority once and for all and act against the Republicans. Failing this, the British would have no difficulty in reasserting their authority in Ireland; thus plans were put in place by the British to attack the Four Courts garrison on 25 June.[3]

Meanwhile, the Four Courts Executive decided to send a detachment of men under the command of Peadar O'Donnell to Northern Ireland, and transport was needed. On 26 June, Leo Henderson, director of the Belfast Boycott, was ordered to raid Ferguson's Garage in Lower Baggot Street.[4] Because both factions of the IRA were united on the northern offensive, it was not expected that the pro-Treaty forces would act against the Republicans, but this was not the case, and a party of National Army troops, under the command of Frank Thornton, raided the garage and arrested Henderson.

That night, in retaliation for Henderson's arrest, a party of men, including Seán MacBride, under the command of Ernie O'Malley, kidnapped the deputy chief-of-staff of the National Army, General J. J. 'Ginger' O'Connell. O'Malley wrote:

> I took a car and three men. We crossed the city and halted a little above McGilligan's [public house] on the opposite side. We saw people enter and depart. After an hour or more I saw Ginger O'Connell leave the house. He walked towards the canal bridge. We followed slowly. The car halted at the bridge. I walked after O'Connell. I touched him on the shoulder.
>
> 'Ginger, you're under arrest,' I said. He turned around quickly. He looked startled. He saw a gun in the hands of a man behind me.
>
> 'Into the car,' I said.
>
> He began: 'What do you mean? I bloody well –'
>
> 'Into the car, quick, Ginger,' I repeated.
>
> He sat down in the back seat, a man on either side … He began to struggle when passing through Westmoreland Street. 'Sit on him,' I said. He was placed on the floor and a man sat on him. As we came through the gate he said: 'I hope they blow the hell out of you.'
>
> I left our prisoner in the guardroom and reported to the Chief of Staff.[5]

The Republicans demanded the release of Henderson in exchange for O'Connell. When their demand was conveyed to

Eoin O'Duffy, chief-of-staff of the pro-Treaty forces, it went unanswered.

As a result of O'Connell's kidnapping, the Provisional Government finally decided to act against the Four Courts garrison. Orders were issued for the Dublin Guards, under the command of Paddy O'Daly, and men from the 2nd Eastern Division, under the command of Tom Ennis, to mobilise a force of approximately 4,000 men. Preparations for an assault on the Four Courts got under way.

CHAPTER 5

27–28 JUNE

On the afternoon of Tuesday 27 June, Provisional Government troops in Crossley Tenders and lorries entered the city's principal streets, namely O'Connell Street, Westmoreland Street, Nassau Street and Dame Street. As the day progressed, more troops entered the city and took up positions around Middle Abbey Street and Henry Street, and directly opposite the Four Courts on the south side of the River Liffey. The pro-Treaty forces took over the Four Courts Hotel in Morgan's Place, less than forty yards away from the main courts' building and the records office. The Bridewell Prison, facing the headquarters block at the rear of the courts, and the nearby medical mission were also taken over. Snipers were placed in St Michan's tower, Church Street, facing the records office, and Jameson's Distillery and a number of tenement houses surrounding the courts were also taken over. As this encirclement was taking place, the men inside the courts could only look on, willing but unable to act because the orders of the Executive were that they were not to be the first to open fire.

Later that evening, Oscar Traynor, O/C Dublin Brigade of the anti-Treaty IRA, received word through a friendly source at Beggars Bush Barracks that the Four Courts was going to be attacked and that he should mobilise his men. Accompanied by Cathal Brugha, Traynor went to the courts to alert the garrison as to what was about to happen, and urged the Executive to evacuate the building and revert to guerrilla tactics, but the Executive refused to leave. Rory O'Connor and Joe McKelvey had by that time begun to write a proclamation, which they gave to Traynor to be printed. Of the sixteen men who signed the proclamation, six were in the courts.[1]

OGLAIGH NA h-EIREANN

PROCLAMATION.

FELLOW CITIZENS OF THE IRISH REPUBLIC.

The fateful hour has come. At the dictation of our hereditary enemy our rightful cause is being treacherously assailed by recreant Irishmen. The crash of arms and the boom of artillery reverberate in this supreme test of the Nation's destiny.

Gallant soldiers of the Irish Republic, stand rigorously firm in its defence, and worthily uphold their noblest traditions. The sacred spirits of the illustrious dead are with us in this great struggle. " Death before Dishonour " being an unchanging principle of our national faith as it was of theirs, still inspires us to emulate their glorious effort.

We therefore appeal to all citizens who have withstood unflinchingly the oppression of the enemy during the past six years to rally to the support of the Republic, and recognise that the resistance now being offered is but the continuance of the struggle that was suspended by the truce with the British. We especially appeal to our former comrades of the Irish Republic to return to that allegiance, and thus guard the Nation's honour from the infamous stigma that her sons aided her foes in retaining a hateful domination over her.

Confident of victory and of maintaining Ireland's Independence, this appeal is issued by the Army Executive on behalf of the Irish Republican Army.

(SIGNED)

Comdt.-Gen. Liam Mellows, Comdt.- Gen. Rory O'Connor, Comdt.-Gen. Jos. McKelvey, Comdt.-Gen. Earnan O'Maille, Comdt.-Gen. Seamus Robinson, Comdt.-Gen. Sean Moylan, Comdt.-Gen. Michael Kilroy, Comdt.-Gen. Frank Barrett, Comdt.-Gen. Thomas Deerig. Comdt. T. Barry, Col.-Comdt. F. O'Faolain, Brig.-Gen. J. O'Connor, Comdt. P. O'Rutiless, Gen. Liam Lynch, Comdt.-Gen. Liam Deasy, Col.-Comdt. Peadar O'Donnell.

28th June 1922.

Failing to persuade the Executive to leave the courts, Traynor and Brugha left the building. Traynor then issued the order for the Dublin Brigade to mobilise.

Unknown to the Provisional Government, by this time relations between the Executive forces in the Four Courts and Liam Lynch and his men from the 1st Southern Division had been re-established. Earlier in the week, Lynch, together with Dick Barrett, quartermaster of the 3rd West Cork Brigade and a veteran of the War of Independence, went with others to the courts; the two opposing Republican sides put aside their differences about the possibility of reuniting the whole army and Lynch was reinstated as chief-of-staff of all the Republican forces. Soon afterwards, Liam Lynch and his men, with the exception of Dick Barrett, who chose to remain in the courts, left the building and went back to their headquarters at the Clarence Hotel, after which they decided to return to Munster.

Inside the Four Courts, the garrison realised just how inadequate their defences were. There were not enough sandbags to barricade the windows, and the various sections in the compound were isolated from each other. To connect the central hall, the headquarters block and the records office, passages had to be made, but again, there were not enough sandbags to make secure passageways. The men had begun to dig a tunnel weeks earlier, beginning at the records office, with the hope of reaching Patterson's match factory in Church Street, but it was not completed and by this time it was waterlogged. In addition to this, they realised they did not have sufficient supplies of food and other basic materials.

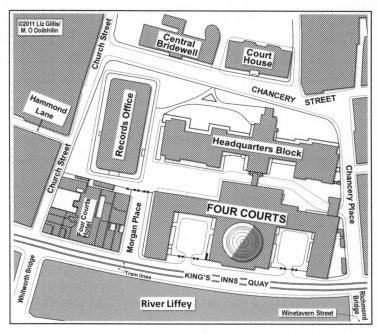

Fig 1. Plan of the Four Courts complex and surrounding area, showing the principal buildings occupied by the opposing forces. N.B. All street names are those of the time.

Paddy O'Brien ordered the men to stand by at their sections. Trenches were dug behind the gates of the courts in case pro-Treaty armoured cars managed to break through. Mines were laid at the front of the building, facing the quays; however, members of the National Army ordered the men who were laying the mines to stop what they were doing.[2] All the garrison could do was to watch, as 'strict orders had been issued not to open fire until fired upon'.[3] Soon afterwards, National Army Lancia cars drove onto the quays and parked outside the gates of the Four Courts, blocking the entrances; again the garrison looked on. Inside the building 'men moved barbed wire, cleaned and checked ammunition, fitted rifle-slings, cleaned rifles, automatics and machine-guns, and laid out spare parts. Captain Paddy O'Brien saw that the officers rechecked the ammunition, examined the weapons, and knew the positions they were to occupy.'[4]

At about 10 o'clock that night, the Provisional Government sent word to the Four Courts Executive that the building was to be evacuated and the garrison were to surrender by midnight. Failure to comply would result in attack. But surrender was not an option for the Executive. In the meantime, pro-Treaty troops under Paddy O'Daly and Tom Ennis continued to surround the courts. Ernie O'Malley described the developing situation:

> Across the river in the darkness men were moving into position. We could see the dark shadows advancing. Armoured cars purred their gentle throttles, heavier Lancias drove up and down. Their troops entered the Four Courts Hotel and the adjoining buildings which fronted part of the Courts. They opened the Bridewell gates, opposite the Headquarters block across the street, and marched in. We could hear them as they prepared the position inside ... Our position was being slowly surrounded. Houses commanding the courtyards and the windows facing the yards were now occupied. The Staters were taking advantage of the fact that we did not want to open fire on them. The Courts was already a trap.[5]

Two eighteen-pounder guns were handed over to Emmet Dalton, director of military operations, National Army, with ten shells for each gun.[6] The guns were placed opposite the courts on the south side of the Liffey at Winetavern Street and

Lower Bridge Street. Midnight came and went, but there was no attack.

The failure of the pro-Treaty forces to attack at this time can be explained by the fact that there was a mutiny of pro-Treaty soldiers at Portobello Barracks. Frank Carney, supplies officer at the barracks, was ordered to hand over weapons and other materials that were to be used in the assault:

> He was about to obey when he recognised the officer receiving them as a British officer from the Phoenix Park depot. Realising that it was in alliance with British against Republicans that he was being called upon to take action, he refused to comply and resigned. Several men resigned with him and all were placed under arrest.[7]

At 3.40 a.m. Tommy 'Skinner' O'Reilly, who was in charge of the guard at the main gate of the Four Courts, received a second ultimatum, which read:

> The officer in charge,
> Four Courts,
>   I, acting under the order of the Government, hereby order you to evacuate the buildings of the Four Courts and to parade your men under arrest, without arms, on that portion of the Quays immediately in front of the Four Courts by 4 a.m.
>   Failing compliance with this order, the building will be taken by me by force, and you and all concerned with you will be held responsible for any life lost or any damage done.
>   By order
>   Thomas Ennis
>   O/C 2nd Eastern Division[8]

O'Reilly took the message to Rory O'Connor who, with the other members of the Executive, was in the central hall under the dome. After some deliberation, O'Reilly was told 'to go back to the gate and tell the dispatch rider there was no reply'.[9]

As 4 a.m. came and went, Paddy O'Daly telephoned the courts for a reply to Ennis' demands, but there was no answer. At 4.10 a.m. on the morning of 28 June, the sound of rifle and machine-gun fire, followed by the thud of bombs exploding, reverberated throughout the city. The Civil War had begun; there was no going back for either side.

CHAPTER 6

WEDNESDAY 28 JUNE

Commandant General Dermot MacManus, director of training, National Army, who was in position at the Phoenix Park side of the courts, believed it was he who fired the opening shots of the battle:

> I went into a house and turned out the people ... Very soon I was in a room with three or four men, and just across the narrow street was this huge building with all the windows sandbagged. I thought it was time we did something and, without realising that there were people covering me there, I took a rifle from one of the men, smashed a window and fired what I believe was the first shot of the battle. It hit a sandbag. A second later, five shots hit the wall behind me. We weren't so rash after that.[1]

Minutes after the opening shots, the eighteen-pounder guns were put into action. The guns were under the command of General Emmet Dalton and Colonel Tony Lawlor. Dalton believed that the guns would be enough to break the Republicans, who were not used to artillery fire. This opinion was shared by many, including John A. Pinkman:

> It was generally believed that the besieged garrison – many of

whom had never been exposed to an armed attack of any sort – would be overawed by the firing of the field guns and the knowledge that they were hemmed in by armed and experienced troops of the National Army, and the affair would be all over within a matter of hours, probably before the next morning.[2]

Nothing could have been further from the truth. First, the gun crews were so inexperienced in using artillery that Dalton himself had to operate one of the guns, staying in position for three hours. Second, the Republicans were not about to surrender and responded to the attack with rifle and machine-gun fire. The Vicker's gun on the captured armoured car, 'The Mutineer', was put to good use against the pro-Treaty snipers in the towers of St Michan's church and Jameson's Distillery. The firing from the Republicans was so intense that Dalton had to use Lancia cars as protective cover for the gun crews.

After about an hour's fighting, the firing subsided. According to Simon Donnelly, who was in the courts:

Free State rang up [the] O/C [Paddy O'Brien] to know if he was going to come out. A very definite reply was given by Captain O'Brien that we were not leaving [the] courts until we were beaten out of it. Attack again opened with terrific fury.[3]

By then the Republicans had realised just how ill-prepared they were for the battle, as O'Malley describes:

Communications between the blocks was in the open. The dome area was cut off from the Headquarters block, the latter from the Records office. The space was covered with rifle and machine-gun fire. One man was hit as he crossed behind me. Paddy O'Brien and I found men to work on a sandbag barricade but there were not enough bags to make a covered bullet-proof passage between the blocks.[4]

When the attack on the Four Courts began, Liam Lynch, with his officers of the 1st Southern Division, were still at the Clarence Hotel. A meeting was summoned for all available officers to attend the hotel, where it was decided that they would go back to their own respective areas and respond to the actions of the Provisional Government with force. Lynch, together with Seán Culhane, Liam Deasy, Con Moylan, Seán Moylan and Moss Twomey, left to get the train back to the south. On their way to Kingsbridge station they were stopped by National Army troops under the command of Liam Tobin, brought to Wellington Barracks on the South Circular Road and held for a time. However, the pro-Treaty forces were unaware that Lynch and his men had healed the divide with the Executive forces in the Four Courts and, on the orders of Richard Mulcahy, the men were released and allowed to continue their journey. Any hope the Provisional Government had of restricting the fighting to Dublin, or indeed of ending the Civil War swiftly, ended with the release of Liam Lynch, chief-of-staff of the Republican forces.[5]

As the morning progressed, the firing continued, with periods of quiet followed by intense intervals of fire from the field guns and machine guns, and the first casualties of the fight were seen. Within an hour of the battle beginning, Volunteer Joseph Considine (anti-Treaty) had been driving along the quays with three other men, making their way towards O'Connell

Street. They encountered a party of National Army troops and in an exchange of fire Considine was shot in the head. He was taken to Jervis Street Hospital and later died of his injury. Soon after this, Volunteer William Long, National Army, was shot in Chancery Street. He, like Considine, was removed to Jervis Street Hospital, and he too succumbed to his wounds.

Inside the courts, the garrison tried to organise themselves, but amid the bombardment it was a futile effort, as O'Malley notes:

> Men of my section [the headquarters section which included the Executive and were in the central hall under the dome] worked picks and shovels to tunnel under the open space whilst some of the section in Headquarters block, tunnelled to meet them … The other tunnel which Rory and the engineers had begun three weeks ago was unfinished … It was originally to have run to Patterson's factory in Church Street. Rory O'Connor had been in charge but the work was not determined. It ran nearly as far as the street and was water-logged … The reserves of each section for counter-attack were very small, and we had no central reserve to fall back on. As I walked about between sections, the buildings seemed to consist chiefly of windows, about five or six windows to each man. They could not all be barricaded; only a few had been made bullet-proof … The roofs were dominated by buildings close to them, and by snipers from St Michan's tower and from the top of Jameson's distillery, but one tunnel was completed by the end of the following day. We could not make another as we could not spare the men. The munitions block containing the records office was isolated. Paddy O'Brien and his adjutant [Seán Lemass] went the rounds frequently during the day, inspecting sections, crossing to munitions which was commanded by the Bridewell prison less

than thirty yards away. The passage was narrow; Thompson guns and machine-guns splattered as they ran across.[6]

At 11 a.m. Captain Mattie McDonnell, Republican forces, was wounded while digging the tunnel connecting the hospital, which was on the ground floor of the headquarters block, to the dome. He was shot in the ankle and conveyed by stretcher to the hospital by Volunteers Mattie Connolly and Vincent Gogan.[7] While the men were carrying McDonnell, they came under fire and in the heat of the moment dropped the stretcher and 'ran and the wounded man got up and ran after them'.[8] While McDonnell was being operated on, the hospital came under heavy fire. McDonnell was removed to another part of the building and was treated successfully.[9]

A number of women were to be found in the courts. Like their colleagues in the IRA, many members of Cumann na mBan were anti-Treaty. These women were invaluable to the Republicans in terms of dispatch-carrying, and more essentially, tending the wounded. Attached to the Four Courts garrison were Máire Comerford, Bridie Clyne, Madge Clifford and Nurse Geraldine O'Donnell. The women worked tirelessly, feeding the men and looking after the wounded in the hospital.

At 2.30 p.m. two shells from across the Liffey struck the front of the courts, creating a huge cloud of dust which almost blocked the Four Courts from view. At this time also, Dalton had received two additional eighteen-pounder guns which were to be put into use on the north side of the Liffey, behind the courts. Under the protection of armoured cars, pro-Treaty troops had dug a trench on the corner of Little Strand Street and Capel Street. A field gun was placed in the trench facing the east side of the courts, and:

> at about 3.30 p.m. this gun fired a shell which struck a lamp post about ten yards away in Little Strand Street, outside Vaughan Bros.' licensed premises, and exploded with terrific force. The lamp post was cut in two, and all the windows and doors in Vaughan's were blown to atoms, and the shop badly wrecked. Windows in Mr Peter Condron's shop on the opposite corner were shattered to pieces and the windows in other shops were also smashed. The gun was removed a few minutes later.[10]

When the attack on the Four Courts began, a simultaneous assault was launched on the Fowler Memorial Hall in Parnell Square. Commandant Frank Bolster, National Army, led the attack. The hall had been held by the Republicans since 25 March and used to house Belfast refugees, but by this time they had been removed to a safer location. The garrison refused to surrender and the attack began at 4 a.m. The hall was heavily barricaded with sandbags and furniture. The National Army attacked the hall with bombs and machine-gun and rifle fire. An armoured car trained its gun on the hall and kept up steady fire at the building. Realising it was impossible to hold the building, the small garrison evacuated the hall, but not before setting the ground floor alight, after which:

> sections of the Fire Brigade were rushed to the scene ... Through the broken windows on the ground floor a regular furnace of flame was revealed, and a big fight was put up by the firemen to subdue the outbreak. The ground floor portion of the structure was

destroyed. While the firemen were conducting their operations, intermittent rifle fire was kept up, but nobody appeared to be injured.[11]

The concert hall beside the Fowler Hall was also destroyed.[12] One soldier was killed in this operation and at least three other people lost their lives.[13]

As soon as the attack on the Four Courts began, Oscar Traynor, O/C Dublin Brigade, summoned the remaining battalions of the anti-Treaty Dublin Brigade to mobilise. The 3rd Battalion, also known as 'Dev's Own', under the command of Joe O'Connor, set up headquarters on the south side of the city at 41 York Street. Traynor had called the various battalions to stand to on 27 June, and some had been dismissed later that night. However, once the fighting began, buildings all over the city were taken over by the Republicans.

Barry's Hotel in Gardiner's Row, previously occupied by the Republicans in March at the time of the convention, had been evacuated, but was now taken over once again by Traynor, who set up his headquarters there. Soon the hotel was full of activity, with volunteers from various battalions presenting themselves to receive orders, including Countess Markievicz, along with a detachment of the Irish Citizen Army. One hundred and twenty-five men and eighteen women of this independent unit turned out once the fighting began, and were attached to the Dublin Brigade. They took orders from Traynor, but had their own chain of command. As well as providing both men and women, the Citizen Army gave Traynor, '3,000 rounds of .303 ammunition', which was badly needed.[14] John Hanratty was commanding officer of the Citizen Army detachment in Barry's Hotel, Countess Markievicz was his second in command. Members of the Citizen Army were sent out to reinforce outposts at 'Vaughan's Hotel in Parnell Square, to Moran's Hotel in Talbot Street, to the Workman's Temperance Club, 41 York Street, to Marrowbone Lane Distillery, and to various other positions around the centre of the city'.[15] Annie Farrington, owner of Barry's Hotel, described what happened next:

> They established their headquarters in the dining room. The first thing they did was to knock all the glass out of the doors and windows. They sandbagged the windows and stuck guns between the bags. They allotted different rooms to the various purposes. They cleared out all the visitors – about forty – giving them barely time to pack their bags. They cleared out the staff, but I refused to go and Miss Keogh and William the Porter stayed with me ... We were not allowed to pass through the rooms they occupied. I can't remember how we put in our time during the occupation. I was half out of my mind thinking of all the money I owed the bank which financed the purchase of the place and now I saw the possibility of the whole place going up in smoke. This was the reason I refused to leave, although they pointed out the risk I was running by staying ... They had the doors barricaded with my good tables and furniture. They did not use the door opposite Rutland Place for fear of being fired on but they opened up the door of the second house. At each side of the inner hall which this door led into they bored holes for guns for the protection of this door.[16]

On the night of 27 June, the main body of the 1st Battalion, who were not in the Four Courts, mobilised at 44 Parnell Square, which had been the original headquarters of the Executive, under the command of Paddy Holohan. Other members of the 1st Battalion were in Fowler's Hall in Parnell Square, Tara Hall in Gloucester Street and No. 5 Blackhall Street, standing to awaiting orders.

Lieutenant Paddy Kelly, 'G' Company, 1st Battalion, in Blackhall Street with his men, was ordered to join the main body at 44 Parnell Square. On arrival they were told to go back to Blackhall Street, presumably to give protection to the Four Courts garrison, who were about to be attacked. Paddy Kelly stated, 'I was instructed not to attack or commit any offensive act unless first attacked; we were to wait at Blackhall Street till we received further orders.'[17] They arrived back at Blackhall Street safely and took over the Gaelic League Hall. Captain Oman, 1st Battalion, was in charge of the section. With the attack on the courts, Oman sent word to Paddy Holohan in 44 Parnell Square, asking what they should do. They were told to stay where they were until notified further.

'C' Company of the 1st Battalion, who were in Tara Hall, were ordered to take over a house at the corner of Strand Street and Capel Street, but they could not move because of the increased troop movement and the shelling of the Four Courts. Realising that it would be almost impossible for his men to get to Strand Street safely, Commandant Holohan ordered 'C' Company to take over Hughes Hotel in Lower Gardiner Street, opposite Moran's Hotel, which had also been occupied. Hughes Hotel consisted of two houses, and Seán Prendergast, O/C of 'C' Company, described how the men prepared the hotel for battle:

> [We] put them in a state of defence, then extended our operations by tunnelling through the adjoining houses until we had taken possession of the line of buildings stretching from the corner of Derrille Place to the corner of Talbot Street. During the progress of that work we had been reinforced by officers and men of two other units, 'E' and 'I' Companies of the First Battalion, as well as a few odd men from different companies … In all the garrison numbered about seventy, forty from 'C' Company.[18]

Four women were also present in Hughes Hotel: Marcella Crimmins, Kathleen Macken, Annie Norgrove and Annie Tobin.[19]

Other buildings occupied were Banba Hall in Parnell Square, 42 North Great George's Street, 35 North Great George's Street (which was the headquarters of Na Fianna, under the command of Seán Harling) and Moran's Hotel, Talbot Street. The pro-Treaty forces took up positions in the National and Provincial Banks on the corner of O'Connell Street and Parnell Street, and a house facing Parnell Street.

As the day progressed, the pro-Treaty forces were finding it difficult to keep up the attack on the courts. Realising that more shells were needed to keep up the assault, Dalton requested more ammunition for the field guns from General Macready, British commander-in-chief, who was stationed in the Royal Hospital, Kilmainham. Macready asked to see Dalton, who arrived at the hospital around 9.30 p.m. They discussed the situation and Dalton emphasised that 'he could not get his men to risk their lives in an assault'.[20] Macready was reluctant to hand over more ammunition as he was not quite certain that the two factions would not unite and use the guns against the

British. After much deliberation, and Dalton's insistence that he would not continue the attack unless given the ammunition, Macready agreed to hand over fifty rounds of shrapnel: 'Which was all we had left, simply to make a noise through the night, as he [Dalton] was afraid that if the guns stopped firing his men would get disheartened and clear off.'[21] And so the attack continued. At intervals of fifteen minutes, the loud explosions of shrapnel shells hitting the Four Courts could be heard all over the city.

As the first days' fighting drew to a close, Máire Comerford tried to get some sleep in the courts, which was almost impossible:

> Liam [Mellows] looking very determined, called Bridie Clyne and I into a great big room where there were two beds in the inside corner, and told us to go asleep. He forbade us from leaving that corner of the room because the rest of it was dangerous … I was still too excited and angry to sleep. But I lay there obediently and watched Liam's small figure as, ignoring the other noises, he moved about on tiptoe. He changed the position of a table, and other things to bring all the amenities he could provide for us into the safety zone. If anybody came to the door he behaved like a nurse in a sick room, shooing them away.[22]

By the day's end, seventeen people were dead, three were wounded, and many more casualties were to follow.

CHAPTER 7

THURSDAY 29 JUNE

As day broke on the morning of 29 June, the noise of the shells hitting the Four Courts could be heard throughout the city. The Republicans had continued to take up strategic positions across the city and harassed the pro-Treaty forces continuously with sniper fire, which intensified as the morning wore on. Unlike the situation on Wednesday, the streets were all but deserted of onlookers. As one reporter commented, 'the sniping seemed to present more terror for the citizen than the massed attack, and the vicious ping of the rifle from a nearby roof sounds more sinister than the boom of the heavy guns'.[1]

That morning, Máire Comerford was called on to carry dispatches to Oscar Traynor. Before leaving the courts she witnessed a poignant scene:

> … when I wheeled my bike to the guardroom door I found the whole floor full of men asleep, in every kind of attitude; some on top of the others. The sun was coming through a deep and narrow hole where a shell had taken part of the corner of the building, without bursting.[2]

Throughout the attack, Comerford was able to get in and out of the Four Courts and carry dispatches to Traynor in O'Connell

Street. The only other people who had such freedom of movement to and from the courts were the members of the Fire Brigade, some of whom were sympathetic to the Republicans, and the ambulance workers.

All the while, the number of casualties mounted. Volunteer George Walsh, National Army, was killed when he was shot in the head while standing at a window in the area near the courts. In the meantime, Emmet Dalton was all too aware that, to enable the pro-Treaty forces to take the courts, they needed to make a breach in the building. However, to do this they needed proper ammunition for the field guns.

That morning, the Royal Hospital, Kilmainham, was hit by a shell coming from the direction of the fighting. Dalton was called on by Macready to investigate and found, 'Ignatius O'Neill … with his gun canted up as he tried to hit a sniper in the dome of the Four Courts. He was using an eighteen-pounder like a rifle and the shells were going right through the dome and landing on the Royal Hospital.'[3]

By the afternoon, the much-needed high-explosive shells arrived from Macready, who had met with Michael Collins to discuss Collins' demands for more weapons and ammunition. While Macready remained reserved about handing over large quantities of arms to Collins, Winston Churchill was more than willing to give the army whatever material they needed, including planes painted green – but flown by British pilots. They were also offered sixty-pound Howitzers. Collins refused both of these offers.

Having received the shells, the attack on the courts intensified. There were three field guns trained on the courts;

two at the front of the building and one at the side, which targeted the records office, where the munitions factory was located. Simon Donnelly recalled:

> No. 3 post overlooking Morgan's Place and in the direction of Guinness Brewery was attacked very vigorously, as was also the orderlies section in the records office facing Church St and Smithfield. Tis well to mention that the orderlies were all members of the Fianna, merely boys and it is to the everlasting credit of that organisation that the fight they put up was by far the stiffest and noblest fight in the courts. That position of the building was a light structure, brick wall and all large windows. A field gun in Smithfield played havoc with that position, as did also enemy garrison [*sic*] in the Four Courts Hotel and Bridewell.[4]

This sentiment about the orderlies section was shared by many, including Seán Lemass, who believed that it was unfair that these very young men had to hold such a position. He felt that older, more experienced men should have at least been in the section with them.[5]

As the firing intensified, the army required a steady supply of ammunition for their weapons. John A. Pinkman, National Army, was one of many soldiers who went on the supply runs from Portobello Barracks to the courts:

> We completed the trip without incident, but when our driver pulled up on the quays in front of the Four Courts so many bullets were ricocheting about that not even a sparrow could have survived in the crossfire. Some of our lads had already reached the perimeter of the building but the Irregulars were fighting

Cathal and Kathleen Brugha with family.
(Courtesy of Topical Press Agency/Kilmainham Gaol Archives)

National Army soldiers rushing up their artillery.
(Courtesy of Topical Press Agency/Kilmainham Gaol Archives)

National Army soldiers crossing O'Connell Street.
(Courtesy of Topical Press Agency/Kilmainham Gaol Archives)

Members of the Four Courts garrison posing with the captured
armoured car 'The Mutineer' in the grounds of the Four Courts.
(Courtesy of Joseph McHenry Collection, Kilmainham Gaol Archives)

Rory O'Connor (standing on car) addressing a public meeting. In the foreground looking at the camera is Peadar Breslin. Both men were later to die in Mountjoy Gaol. *(Courtesy of Peadar Breslin)*

Joe McKelvey, member of the Four Courts Executive and assistant chief-of-staff, Republican forces. *(Courtesy of Kilmainham Gaol Archives)*

Brigadier-General Paddy O'Daly with his wife.
(Courtesy of Kilmainham Gaol Archives)

William Doyle (standing)
after the takeover of the Four
Courts, April/May 1922.
*(Courtesy of Liam Doyle, c/o
Kilmainham Gaol Archives)*

Lieutenant Paddy Kelly, 'G'
Company, 1st Battalion, Dublin
Brigade, Republican forces.
(Courtesy of Paddy Kelly)

Two pro-Treaty snipers, possibly at the rear of the Four Courts, Dublin. *(Courtesy of Topical Press/Kilmainham Gaol Archives)*

Members of the Fire Brigade putting out a fire at the rear of the Four Courts. *(Courtesy of Ray Broe)*

National Army soldiers trying to gain entry into the Gresham Hotel.
(Courtesy of Ray Broe)

Cathal Brugha lying-in-state, surrounded by members of Cumann
na mBan, at the Mater Hospital, Dublin.
(Courtesy of Kilmainham Gaol Archives)

National Army soldiers trying to gain entry into the Gresham via James W. Mackey's shop, O'Connell Street. *(Courtesy of Ray Broe)*

National Army soldiers at the bottom of Henry Street firing the eighteen-pounder gun at the Republican stronghold in the 'Block'. *(Courtesy of Kilmainham Gaol Archives)*

Attack on the Four Courts, 28–30 June 1922.
(Courtesy of Mercier Press)

Armoured lorry with graffiti chalked on its side, 'We have no time for Trucers'. *(Courtesy of Topical Press/Kilmainham Gaol Archives)*

desperately and our boys were running short of ammunition. We had to take the boxes of ammo right up to the fellows who were firing, but to avoid being hit by the Irregulars we had to crouch as low as possible as we ran forward. Our lads were tired and dirty, and they were as badly in need of a drink of water as they were of ammunition.[6]

While returning to Portobello Barracks, Pinkman's lorry was attacked by Republicans. The driver of the lorry was wounded in the arm but there were no fatalities.[7]

Throughout the day a number of people, including Maud Gonne MacBride and other women, appealed to both sides to end the fighting. This was all to no avail, as the Provisional Government demanded complete surrender by the Republicans, and that they must surrender their arms, which the Republicans refused to do. Meanwhile, Oscar Traynor ordered John Hanratty, Citizen Army, who was in Barry's Hotel, to take thirty men with him and seize the Hamman Hotel on the east side of O'Connell Street, which was to be used as Traynor's new headquarters. Hanratty made his way to the Hamman:

> The party had to pass the Parnell statue, where a Free State armoured car was stationed, and so had to run the gauntlet of enemy fire … With experienced officers in front and behind to keep them together, they managed to get through the danger zone. As soon as the Citizen Army group reached the hotel they had the task of putting it in a state of defence.[8]

They soon realised that they did not have enough materials to defend the ground floor of the hotel, the entrance of which was quite wide. If they came under attack from an armoured car they would not stand a chance against its firepower. Sandbags were needed, but there were none available. It was suggested that ashes from the boiler in the basement of the hotel could be wrapped in sheets and used, but these would be useless against machine-gun fire. However, in the Tramway Office next to the Hamman, which was also held by the Republicans, there was plenty of material – trunks and bags of all sizes – that could be used. A commandeering party was sent to the office and with the material obtained they successfully barricaded the entrance to the Hamman.

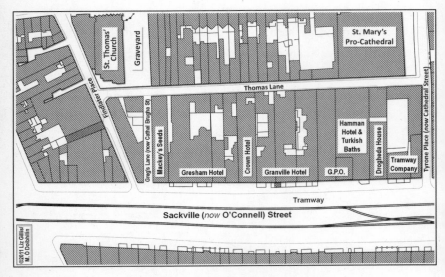

Fig. 2: Plan of O'Connell Street, featuring the Block (from Mackey's Seeds to the Tramway Company) and other buildings involved in the fighting.
N.B. All street names are those of the time. Where relevant, modern names are given in brackets.

Other buildings seized by the Republicans on the orders of Traynor were the Sackville Street Club, O'Connell Street; CYMS premises, North Frederick Street; the Minerva Hotel; Messrs Beckett, Walsh & Co.; Banba Hall; Rutland High School (all in the vicinity of Parnell Square); the Carlisle Building on D'Olier Street; the Swan Hotel/public house, Aungier Street; Messrs Craig, Gardiner and Co., Dame Street; and a corner house on Dolphin's Barn/South Circular Road.[9] Moran's Hotel, opposite Hughes Hotel had been taken over and was under the command of Liam O'Doherty, O/C 5th Battalion (Engineers). Traynor's hope was that he could get some units from the various outposts to make their way to the Four Courts to relieve the garrison who were now continuously under fire, but this action never really materialised, as Laurence Nugent, quartermaster of the 3rd Battalion stated:

> During the first few days in York Street the atmosphere was rather monstrous. The Four Courts was being bombarded from two points and while men were prepared to attempt an attack for their relief, they were not allowed to move. Then the outlying posts were called in and we expected the relief attack, but it never came … We had not the arms, but the men were prepared to act with what they had.[10]

Soon after the Hamman was taken, Traynor and his headquarters staff made their way to the building, leaving behind a small garrison to hold Barry's Hotel. With him were Cathal Brugha, Éamon de Valera, Seán T. O'Kelly and Austin Stack, who had all turned out for mobilisation as soon as the attack on the Four Courts began. Brugha was promoted to the rank of commandant by Traynor and was put in charge of what was to become known as the 'Block'.[11] Throughout the day there was much activity in this area between the opposing forces. The Republicans raided the grocery premises of Messrs Findlater's, Dorset Street and succeeded in commandeering supplies of food.

Despite the fighting on O'Connell Street becoming more intense, some aspects of everyday civilian life continued. Ordinary people still attended mass at the pro-cathedral, Marlborough Street, albeit under continuous fire. As one reporter remarked, 'Snipers became active on the roofs of houses all round the area, and again the tragic spectacle was witnessed of ambulances passing to and fro with wounded to the hospitals.'[12]

Many streets surrounding the Republican outposts had been mined, most notably the street outside Moran's Hotel and Derrille Place, near Hughes Hotel. The garrison in Hughes watched as armoured cars drove near the mine, but they did not come close enough and so the mine lay on the road untouched. Seán Prendergast recalled what it was like to witness the excitement that was caused in Hughes Hotel while the garrison looked on: 'Manoeuverings [sic] like that intrigued our men, who gradually worked themselves into a frenzy hoping that the next time the mine will [sic] blow the car to blazes.'[13] Moran's Hotel stood across the road, on the corner of Talbot Street. The garrison was ordered by Liam O'Doherty to bore holes into adjacent houses, thus connecting them all together.

Annie M. P. Smithson was one of the women sent to Moran's to carry out first aid duties. She described the scene in Moran's: 'We nurses and the Cumann na mBan occupied the big basement of the hotel, using a large kitchen for the cooking, and several smaller rooms for dressings and other needs.'[14]

In the meantime, the pro-Treaty forces had taken up positions in Amiens Street Station, where a sniper was placed in the clock tower. Talbot House and the North Star Hotel, also in Amiens Street, and the Model Schools in Gardiner Street were also held by the National forces.

As the day wore on, Seán Prendergast in Hughes Hotel received orders from Paddy Holohan that his men were to leave the hotel and move to Scott's in Upper O'Connell Street, where they would be nearer to headquarters. This would have left O'Doherty and his men in Moran's in an almost impossible position, as they would have been unable to hold the area successfully by themselves. O'Doherty was superior in rank to Prendergast, but up to that point he had not imposed his authority on Prendergast and his men. However, O'Doherty could not stand by and do nothing, and declared to Prendergast, 'If you go we move also.'[15] Prendergast, though unwilling to disobey O'Doherty, had received his orders from Holohan, who was O/C of the battalion, so he set about moving his men. O'Doherty and his men still threatened to leave, and in an effort to decide what should be done, Prendergast sent two messengers – Marcella Crimmins and Annie Tobin – to the Hamman Hotel to get an answer from Oscar Traynor; 'the answer was simple and terse, "place yourself under the orders of Commandant O'Doherty"'.[16] Thankfully there were no hard feelings between the two garrisons.

Word soon reached the men that the pro-Treaty forces were holding Talbot House and, even more seriously, the Model

Schools. The Model Schools building presented the most danger to the Republicans, as a portion of that building:

> reached to the rear of the houses occupied by us. Had we men and guns available, those buildings would have been in our possession from the beginning. Under the circumstances we had to accept the situation to our dire disadvantage.[17]

Back at the Four Courts, the battle was raging. As well as artillery fire, the Provisional Government forces used Lewis guns, Hotchkiss guns and Thompson sub-machine guns to batter the building. The Republicans had machine guns and rifles on the roof of the courts, but they were no match for the pro-Treaty force's arsenal. The west wing of the Four Courts at Morgan's Place and, more importantly, the records office, were by now badly damaged. The crew of 'The Mutineer' did their best to beat back the onslaught, but with great difficulty, as Simon Donnelly recounted:

> On Thursday, the Vickers gun [of the car] was put out of action during a duel between the crew of [the] car and the Four Courts Hotel garrison. This was a serious handicap, but after some hours a Lewis gun was rigged up, and it went again into action. During this time the enemy artillery was paying us great attention.[18]

Among all this chaos, the men were trying to tunnel across to the munitions block beneath the cellars. This work was carried out under the supervision of Simon Donnelly, who was in the headquarters block. The headquarters staff held a meeting to discuss what to do. Eventually they decided not to attack the garrison in the Four Courts Hotel, even though, if this was successful, it could relieve some of the pressure on the orderlies section. Instead, they decided to lay mines all over the court-yards in the event of the pro-Treaty forces storming the building. Paddy O'Brien was not happy with this decision, and he decided that the only option was to burn the records office so that it could not be used as a base by attacking pro-Treaty troops, after the section had been safely withdrawn.

The garrison in the records office had by now retreated to the only place that gave some protection from the barrage of fire: the ground floor at the rear of the building facing the dome of the central hall. Lieutenant Ned Kelleher was ordered by O'Brien to evacuate the orderlies section and set the building alight. While making his way to the records office, Kelleher was suddenly stopped in his tracks; standing in front of him was a National Army soldier. Unknown to the Republicans, the pro-Treaty forces had gained access to the grounds of the Four Courts. Kelleher was placed under arrest.[19]

For hours the field guns bombarded the building. Eventually a breach was made at Morgan's Place, but it was not big enough and they needed to widen the gap for the soldiers to get through. However, in trying to do so an inexperienced gunner on the south side of the Liffey lowered the field gun too much and blew a hole in the Liffey wall.[20] To widen the breach Colonel Tony Lawlor, from his position in Winetavern Street, intensified his efforts and with the other two field guns they unleashed a barrage of fire on the courts. Peadar MacMahon, who commanded another eighteen-pounder gun, was in position in Green Street at the rear of the courts. By that time, approximately 2,000 troops surrounded the Four Courts. As the firing continued, storming parties made their way across the Liffey and, under the cover of heavy fire, attempted to take the building.

One party under the command of Commandant Joe McGuinness and Commandant Patrick O'Connor was successful in entering the complex on the Church Street side, gaining entry to the records office and arresting the garrison, which numbered thirty-three Volunteers. It was during this assault that Volunteers Tom Wall and John (Seán) Cusack, both members of the orderlies section, were fatally wounded. It seems that they were involved in digging a tunnel to connect the records office to the headquarters block when the building was stormed: 'they were given no chance to surrender, both of them were fired on and mortally wounded, dying in a few hours after capture'.[21]

Another storming party, led by Commandant Joe Leonard, was not so fortunate. They had to make their way along the front of the courts on the quays to access the breach in the western wing. Coming under heavy fire from a Lewis gun, they made their way slowly and Commandant Leonard was wounded. He was succeeded by Commandant General Dermot MacManus who, together with Emmet Dalton, was successful in entering the breach. During this assault, three National Army soldiers were killed and fourteen wounded.

Slowly but surely the pro-Treaty forces were making progress, but at a cost. As the second day of fighting ended, nine more people were dead and another twenty-three had been wounded.

CHAPTER 8

FRIDAY 30 JUNE

In the early hours of Friday morning, the bombardment of the Four Courts continued fiercely. The National Army was determined to bring the battle to a conclusion. The courts were being hit from three points: Winetavern Street and Lower Bridge Street facing the courts on the Liffey, and Hammond Lane at the side.

Inside the Four Courts, the situation was becoming desperate. The men were tired and hungry, and it was only a matter of time before the whole building would be stormed. The headquarters section, in the central hall under the dome, hurriedly set about barricading the area. Whatever was at hand was used: barbed wire, furniture, mine cases, rubble, anything that might give some protection. The area was also mined.

All the while, the crew of 'The Mutineer' did their best to hold back the advancing pro-Treaty forces, firing round after round at the west wing, trying to locate the enemy. Paddy O'Brien tried in vain to put forward a proposal to the headquarters staff for a counter-attack. He had laid mines which, if detonated, would blow a hole in the building, forming a barricade of sorts. The surrounding area was also mined; the plan was to detonate these mines, thus holding back the attacking forces. This plan, like so many before, was also rejected by the headquarters staff,

Rory O'Connor's reply to O'Brien being, '"If you do [detonate the mines] you'll make a big hole in the building" and Paddy saluted and went off.'[1]

In the meantime, Paddy O'Brien's brother Dinny with two of his friends, Joseph Page and Cathal 'Chummy' Hogan, left the dome area armed with a Lewis gun, to see if they could locate any pro-Treaty soldiers. Ernie O'Malley followed them, his mood very different from theirs:

'This is great gas,' said Chummy, as we picked our way slowly up a jet-black corridor … Where did these men inherit their gay insouciance, as if war was an everyday, trivial matter, and why was I up here, I thought again, as Chummy stood up to fire.[2]

None of the enemy were found.

It was hoped by the Four Courts garrison that some of Oscar Traynor's men would break through the pro-Treaty force's cordon to relieve them. This, in reality, was never going to happen, as the main body of Traynor's forces were entrenched on the east side of O'Connell Street, which was not the ideal location for any assault on the courts. Traynor's men were also hemmed in by increasing fire from the pro-Treaty forces. The Four Courts garrison were completely isolated. Ernie O'Malley commented: 'We had about fifty rounds per rifle now; there were five Thompson guns with numerous drums but not so much ammunition, two Lewis guns and the Vickers.'[3]

The headquarters staff held another meeting. Again, O'Brien put forward a plan, this time about how to evacuate the building. His plan was to lead a party of men, under the protection of 'The

Mutineer', out of the courts and fight their way to Mary's Abbey, where they might have a chance to meet up with Traynor's men. As before, he was overruled. Their decision was to stay – they felt if they abandoned the Four Courts it would be believed by some that they were abandoning the Republic: 'There was a silence for a while. Paddy O'Brien became the disciplined deferential soldier again. "We'd best strengthen our side of the building," he said, "and prepare to receive an attack."'[4] Rory O'Connor believed that at first light they could make their way through the sewers and in turn avoid the pro-Treaty forces and withdraw the garrison safely. Liam Mellows was reluctant to leave and there was a difference of opinion between the members of the Executive. As dawn broke, however, it was discovered that the sewers had flooded: there was nothing to do but wait for the inevitable onslaught.

Soon enough, the shelling and gunfire intensified; 'the boom of the field guns operating against the Four Courts resounded all over Dublin'.[5] 'Ginger' O'Connell, whose kidnapping by the Republicans had initiated the attack on the courts, was now placed in the central hall, underneath the dome, and kept out of harm's way.

In the ensuing attack, Paddy O'Brien was wounded in the head by splinters of glass. He passed command over to Ernie O'Malley, saying, 'I want you to take charge now Ernie … I can't think clearly any more. But I wish we had tried to fight our way through last night.'[6]

Soon afterwards, a ceasefire was called to allow the wounded in the Four Courts to be removed. They had been removed from the hospital on the ground floor of the headquarters block to the dome area of the building some time earlier, under heavy fire. A ceasefire had been requested the previous day, but this was refused by Brigadier-General Paddy O'Daly, who insisted the wounded would be let out only as prisoners. By this time, however, it was too dangerous to keep them in the building. After the wounded had been removed from the courts, firing resumed with even greater intensity.

The crew in 'The Mutineer' were still battling away, trying desperately to hold back the attacking forces. Eventually though, the armoured car was put out of action when General Dermot MacManus, National Army, blew the tyres with his Lewis gun. The crew of 'The Mutineer' had no option but to abandon the car. With this last line of protection gone, it was evident to those in the courts that the end was near.

By 11 a.m. a fire had broken out in the headquarters block at the rear of the courts. Simon Donnelly, who was in this area, noted:

> Incendiary bombs [were] thrown into GHQ Block in which the chemicals shop took fire owing to the inflammable substances in the building. The fire made great headway. Orders were issued to all men to retire to the other side of the courts, that is the portion next to the quay. They got over by means of a tunnel which had been dug under the road ... I was directed to see this portion of the building clear and myself and Fr Dominic were the last to leave it.[7]

Meanwhile, in O'Connell Street, Oscar Traynor tried desperately to get detachments of men to the Four Courts. Paddy Kelly, had by this time made his way to 44 Parnell Square with some of his men. They were gathered by Commandant Paddy Holohan, and around twenty men from different companies were chosen to act as a relief unit, their aim being to get to the Four Courts. The plan was that Holohan would lead the party; however, while making their way through Mary Street, Volunteer Thomas Markey, 'G' Company, 1st Battalion was shot and later died of his wounds. The men returned to 44 Parnell Square, and again they attempted to move out, this time their goal being 'Jenkin's' (most likely Jenkinsons Auctioneers) in Capel Street. Holohan again led the main body, with Paddy Kelly and his party of fifteen men following about twenty minutes later. They were to proceed to Jenkin's via Parnell Street. Paddy Kelly described their journey:

I marched in single line with half my men on each side of the street. When approaching Stafford Street we were attacked by machine-gun fire and two of my men had their hats shot off but were not wounded. I shouted to the men to take cover in the doorways and we returned the fire for about five minutes but we were not quite sure of the enemy's location. After about ten minutes I gave the order to advance, this time making use of what cover we could find, and proceeding by short rushes. In this manner we safely reached Ryder's Row, a short street leading from Parnell Street to Capel Street. At this point there was a terrific explosion and a column of smoke and flame shot several hundred feet into the air. The Four Courts had blown up. The explosion shattered windows all around us and debris of all sorts fell in the street. I halted my party under cover opposite Jenkin's. We had to cross Capel Street under fire from an armoured car and a party of Free State troops stationed near the corner of Mary's Lane and Parnell Street. I sent my men across the street in two's

and three's [sic] at intervals of from three to five minutes. We got
through with one man slightly wounded.[8]

Around the time that Kelly and his men were making their way
to the Four Courts, Traynor ordered John Hanratty, Citizen
Army, to assemble a group of men and take over Dobson's public
house and Griffith's boot shop on the corner of Abbey Street and
Capel Street, only 400 yards from the courts. With him went
George Norgrove, Jim Keogh, Richard McCormack, Joe Kelly
and Thomas O'Neill, all Citizen Army men. Two Volunteers and
four women (two from Cumann na mBan and Annie Flinter and
Diana Hunter, both attached to the Citizen Army) accompanied
them. The women were vital to the group: they could carry the
guns, as they would look less suspicious. Opposite Dobson's was
a pro-Treaty outpost in Moran and Flynn's clothing shop. Hanratty was ordered not to draw any attention from the enemy, as
he recalled, 'no barricade or defence must be constructed until
the last minute … The idea was to lie low and create a diversion
to cover the rush from the Four Courts when it came.'[9]

In Dobson's, Hanratty found the owner, the barmen, a cus-
tomer and the cook. They were ordered to carry on as normal as
the sentry in Moran and Flynn's had a clear view of the premises.
However, before Hanratty could do anything, the Four Courts
exploded:

> Along the road and the pavement, driven by the force of the
> explosion came hurtling piles of law books, papers, documents
> which had lain undisturbed for years in the Four Courts. They
> bounded along, making a noise like a charging army.[10]

Back at the Four Courts, there were scenes of utter carnage. Soldiers lay wounded and there was debris scattered all over the area. But what had happened? It seems that the fire, which had started in the headquarters block, had spread quickly to the records office and the munitions factory, where *at least* two tonnes of gelignite and other explosive materials were stored. At 11.45 a.m. the Fire Brigade received a call from Paddy O'Daly alerting them to the fact that the Four Courts was on fire. Captain Myers, chief of the Fire Brigade, refused to send his men unless a ceasefire was called; O'Daly refused to do this, saying 'Ireland is more important than the fire at the Four Courts.'[11] By noon the fire was raging. The Fire Brigade did make its way to the courts, but there was little that could be done. Soon afterwards, a shell struck the building and at 12.30 p.m., 'There was a thunderous roar and a blinding flash of flame, straight up into the sky for about 500 feet.'[12]

The *Irish Life* newspaper reported:

> A few minutes later, fragments of legal documents, urged into the sky by the explosion, were rained in several parts of the city … The explosion took place under the offices of the probate and land judges' courts, completely demolishing that wing of the building and throwing myriads of forms and documents into the sky.[13]

Máire Comerford, who was in the courts at the time of the explosion, said: 'The shock blew me back, the full length of my arms, then forward again, while dust and fragments scattered everywhere.'[14] At least fifty pro-Treaty troops and five Republicans were wounded in the explosion; miraculously none of them were killed. Quietness descended over the area, and during this lull in the fighting the ambulance crews worked tirelessly to remove the wounded from the courts. Joe Connolly, a member of the Fire Brigade, but also a member of the Citizen Army, went to the courts to remove the wounded. His younger brother George had been in the Four Courts during the attack but managed to make his way out of the building. Paddy O'Brien, though wounded, refused to leave his men. Máire Comerford recalled:

> We had to squash together in a ring around the argument between Paddy and the others. He did not want to go. Eventually he said he was O/C and no one there could give him orders. But Liam [Mellows] (I think) told him that because he was wounded and unable to command any further … he must accept the decision to send him out. It was an order.[15]

By then the courts were becoming untenable. The central hall had been mined, and the shelling was about to begin again. The men retreated to the last habitable section of the building – the cellars, under the library near Chancery Street, on the east side of the complex.

By 1 p.m. the firing and shelling resumed, and by 2.15 p.m. two more explosions had ripped through the main area of the courts, the central hall underneath the dome, again throwing centuries-old documents all over the city skyline. In this explosion, Firemen King, Gaffney and Seaver were wounded and removed to hospital.

Inside the courts, with the building crumbling around them, the garrison discussed what they should do. The headquarters staff, including Rory O'Connor and Liam Mellows, were in favour of surrendering, while others, including Ernie O'Malley, wanted to continue the fight, or at least to try to make their way out of the building. Soon afterwards, a message got through from Oscar Traynor, reading:

To: Acting Chief of Staff, Four Courts

I have gone into the whole situation re your position, and have studied the same very carefully, and I have come to the following conclusion: To help me to carry on the fight outside you must surrender forthwith. I would be unable to fight my way through to you even at terrific sacrifice. I am expecting reinforcements at any moment.

If the Republic is to be saved your surrender is a necessity.

As Senior Officer outside I take it that I am entitled to order you to make a move which places me in a better military position. This order must be carried out without discussion. I will take full responsibility.

O. Traynor

O/C Dub[16]

No further discussion was needed. Fr Albert, who had come to the Four Courts to remove the wounded, acted as a mediator between the two sides. He met Paddy O'Daly in the Four Courts Hotel to discuss terms of surrender. O'Daly's response was that nothing but unconditional surrender was acceptable. Fr Albert returned to the men with O'Daly's response. He was then sent back to O'Daly to see if terms could be agreed for the ordinary rank and file Volunteers; there was no reply.

Simon Donnelly recalled what happened next:

A short time afterwards Liam Mellowes [*sic*], Joe McKelvey, Ernie O'Malley, with tears in their eyes addressed the men stating that to save the lives of such men they had decided to surrender. They informed the men that surrender was no dishonour, while they were compelled to surrender their guns, they would never surrender their principles. It was only by joint appeal the men were held in check.[17]

Before they left the building, orders were given that all arms were to be given to the officers and destroyed. Peadar Breslin, who had been supplies officer in the Four Courts, and Ernie O'Malley were involved in this work. Guns were stripped, broken and piled together, then doused with paraffin and set alight. O'Malley, as O/C of the garrison, led the surrender. A bugler sounded the ceasefire order, and Brigadier-General O'Daly and his staff made their way to Chancery Place on the east side of the courts.

As the beleaguered garrison made their way out of the building, Peadar Breslin, noticing that the men were overcome with emotion, said to them, 'Wipe your faces … I can see the lines of the tears.'[18] At the head of the group were O'Malley, Liam Mellows and Rory O'Connor. Colonel Tony Lawlor, National Army, took the men to Ormond Quay and later said of them, 'They were disappointed and upset, and some of them were holding on to each other.'[19] O'Malley then ordered his men to fall in, in files of two. At 4 p.m. on the afternoon of 30 June, the Four Courts garrison formally surrendered.

By this time, curious onlookers had begun to emerge to witness the scene. As one newspaper reporter noted:

Comdt.-Gen. [*sic*] A. [Tony] Lawlor and Ernest O'Malley moved up and down the lines, and after a short discussion the first company, about 30 strong, headed by Ernest O'Malley, Liam Mellows, Rory O'Connor, and Seán MacBride, was called to attention. With two lines of armed troops filed along each side, and headed by an armoured car, the prisoners were marched off to Jameson's Distillery. The other company, which numbered about 100, remained for some time, and four of them produced a Tricolour flag and waved it aloft.[20]

Over 140 men of the Four Courts garrison surrendered to the pro-Treaty forces. Compared to the pro-Treaty forces, who had suffered losses of at least seven killed and upwards of seventy wounded, the Republicans suffered relatively few casualties in the battle of the Four Courts: three volunteers were killed and eight wounded. As they marched wearily towards Jameson's Distillery there stood behind them a shell of what had once been a magnificent building. For many of these men the fight was over, but for those under Oscar Traynor's command, and more sadly, the ordinary citizens, the war was just beginning.

CHAPTER 9

FRIDAY 30 JUNE
TO SATURDAY 1 JULY

From midday on Friday 30 June, the fighting around O'Connell Street and the other Republican-held areas intensified. Pro-Treaty forces were now in possession of the Ballast Office on the corner of Westmoreland Street and Aston Quay, which gave them commanding views of the whole length of O'Connell Street. Snipers were placed on the roof of the building. In particular, in the areas of Amiens Street, Gardiner Street and Talbot Street, the firing was more concentrated. Pro-Treaty troops scoured the streets, many of which had been mined.[1] Attached to these patrols, for obvious reasons of safety, was at least one armoured car. The mine that had been laid by the Moran's Hotel garrison still lay on the road, untouched. In Hughes Hotel, the garrison, now aware that the Four Courts had fallen, waited for the inevitable attack on their outpost. They were practically cut off from headquarters in the Hamman and had no plan of action; indeed, they did not know if one existed, as Seán Prendergast stated:

Our role, if we were to take our orders literally, was purely defensive ... It would be foolhardy to expect that we would last as much as one day's substantial bombardment should the Treaty forces bring into play sufficiently large forces and equivalent material, which they so lavishly possessed, against us … If they were truly cognisant of our many weaknesses … they would have come to close quarters with us sooner.[2]

Meanwhile over at Jenkin's in Capel Street, Paddy Kelly, who with his men had been on their way to the Four Courts when it exploded, waited for orders that were not forthcoming. Commandant Paddy Holohan was in command, but the garrison were disorganised, with only a few men on guard duty, even though pro-Treaty forces, under the command of Commandant James Slattery, were rapidly surrounding Capel Street.

Inside the building, the men discussed what they could do, but no agreement was reached. Kelly, together with Section-Commander Paddy Dalton, took it upon themselves to inspect the premises to see if they could be held, or if indeed there was any way of escape; all they discovered was that they were easy targets for the pro-Treaty forces who were now surrounding the area. By the time the two men returned to the main area of Jenkin's, they discovered that Commandant Holohan had left, leaving Vice-Commandant Irvin in charge, and he decided that their best option was to surrender. Neither Kelly nor Dalton were happy with this decision but they were unwilling to disobey orders. However, they would not surrender their weapons and both men hid their guns in the basement of Jenkin's. Dalton managed to escape from the building, but Kelly and the others were arrested by Slattery. They were taken first to Wellington Barracks and later to Mountjoy Gaol. Dalton and some other men from 'G' Company were later arrested. As a result of the operations in Capel Street, fifty Republicans were arrested by Slattery.[3]

After the fall of the Four Courts, some of the women who had been in the building at one time or another managed to make their way to the Hamman Hotel. Moira Kennedy O'Byrne described what she found when she arrived there:

> Holes had been bored between it [the Hamman] and other buildings as far as the Gresham. We were very hungry and started looking for food. Some of the men said, 'Come on, we'll dine at the Gresham, follow me.' It was a long trek crawling on our tummies through the holes in the walls at different levels. We arrived at the Gresham and found the tables in the dining-room laden with food which had been abandoned by the hastily departed guests.[4]

John A. Pinkman, who was involved in the round-up operations, described how the operations were carried out:

> ... many of the Irregulars still at large in Dublin set up a number of outposts and sniper positions throughout the city ... As soon as we located such outposts it seldom took much effort to flush them out. We'd simply rush to the house in a tender, kick down the door and arrest the startled 'defenders'.[5]

Though this was certainly true in many cases, when it came to the 'defenders' in the Block and the outposts in and around Talbot Street, removing them was not such an easy task.

CHAPTER 10

SATURDAY 1 JULY

Saturday morning began with an air of normality. Civilians, though not great in number, went hurriedly about their business, and trams were seen operating near the city. However, by the afternoon the streets were once again empty, save for the Red Cross ambulances and doctors' vehicles, and once more the sound of rifle and machine-gun fire could be heard. Barricades had by that time been erected throughout the city centre; mainly in Talbot Street, Railway Street, Marlborough Street and Waterford Street. A reporter for the *Sunday Independent* newspaper wrote: 'These barricades were built up from all sorts and conditions of contrivances, vehicular and otherwise, ranging from the domestic washtub in Marlborough St to the gilded char-a-banc in Railway St.'[1]

In addition to the buildings they already held, the Republicans had also taken over Dominick Street House, the Rotunda – which gave commanding views of the crossroads at Parnell Street and O'Connell Street – the Corporation Workshops in Stanley Street, the Pawn Office in Gardiner Street, near Hughes Hotel and a number of buildings in Harcourt Street.

The expected attack on Moran's Hotel and Hughes Hotel began early on Saturday morning. It started after an armoured car carrying pro-Treaty troops came under heavy fire from the men in Moran's, after which the mine near the hotel was detonated as the car passed by. No one was injured in the blast, but a determined effort was then put up by the pro-Treaty forces to clear the area of Republicans. Immediately, barricades were erected in Amiens Street, Talbot Street and Beresford Place:

> Vehicles of every description were commandeered, particularly horse vehicles. The drivers were ordered to stop and the horses unyoked. The vehicles were then placed across the street about 30 yards on the Amiens St side of the hotel. A double barricade was also erected a little further down. The entrance from Beresford Place to Talbot St was cut off by vehicles being placed under the bridge in Lr Gardiner St ... Carts, cars, and all classes of vehicles were commandeered, and a barricade erected at the junction of Gloucester St, Findlater Place, and Marlborough St. Strong barricades have also been erected at Mabbot Lane, leading from Talbot St to Railway and Gloucester Streets.[2]

The garrisons were by then completely surrounded.

The blast from the Moran's mine had a damaging effect on the defences at Hughes Hotel. Seán Prendergast described it:

> ... tumbling down a lot of our barricades at doors and windows and causing the buildings to quiver and shake. So violent was its impact that several of us were knocked to the ground ... What a mess it left our position in. With our defences broken down and strewn about the rooms and in the hallways, our positions presented anything but a fortress then.[3]

In nearby Stanley Street, the Republicans in the Corporation Workshops tried to hold their position but, under increasing rifle fire, the buildings were taken and the men arrested. At Barry's Hotel, the garrison were busy preparing the building for the expected attack. They bored holes on both sides of the hotel into neighbouring houses, to provide them with an escape route. But Annie Farrington, the owner of the hotel, still refused to leave.

In O'Connell Street, the pro-Treaty forces occupied buildings in the lower part of the street, while in the Block, Oscar Traynor and his men worked tirelessly to prepare their position for defence. Seán Dowling, 4th Battalion, was in the Tramway Office, on the corner of Cathedral Street and Upper O'Connell Street. He was O/C of the 4th Battalion, who in the main were anti-Treaty, but until the fighting broke out he had not committed himself to taking up arms. As he stated:

> I had no great reverence or trust in our leadership; still less in the Provisional Government of Mr Griffith. Anyway, I was very undecided myself … I was still in that mood when against my struggling conscience, I found myself behind the barrel of a gun in Upper O'Connell Street.[4]

Dowling had thirty Volunteers under his command, including Todd Andrews, another member of the 4th Battalion, who had arrived at the Hamman after the Four Courts had fallen. He was handed a rifle and a Thompson sub-machine gun and given his position:

... in a top window of the old Tramway Company office, which, being on a corner site, gave me a complete view of O'Connell Street as far as Westmoreland Street ... I found that the other members of the garrison ... were all members of the Fourth Battalion.[5]

Robert 'Bobby' Bonfield was also a member of the garrison in the Tramway Office.[6] Members of Cumann na mBan supported the men. The Tramway Office was barricaded and holes had been bored in the walls:

... between all the houses, shops and hotels in the block. It was possible to move freely from Lipton's in Earl Street to the Gresham Hotel. This meant that we, the occupying troops, were supplied with the necessities – even luxuries – of life in abundance. We had deep mattresses, thick blankets ... joints of lamb, boxes of chocolates, Turkish or Egyptian cigarettes at choice or any other brand we wanted.[7]

Andrews could see the Ballast Office clearly from his position, and it was not long before the fight began between the two opposing garrisons. The fight continued for some time, and the position of those in the Tramway Office looked set to worsen that evening with the appearance of an armoured car at the corner of Henry Street directly opposite Andrews' position. The section came under heavy fire from the armoured car, but suffered no casualties.

The garrison in the Block itself numbered seventy men and thirty women, including Oscar Traynor (Brigade O/C), Cathal Brugha (O/C of the garrison in the Block and the O'Connell

Street area), Éamon de Valera, Robert Barton, Austin Stack, Countess Markievicz, Nurse Linda Kearns, Kathleen Barry and Muriel MacSwiney.[8] In all, the Block consisted of fourteen buildings, connected together into one vast fortified structure:

> The main positions from Cathal Brugha Street [formally Greg's Lane] down to Cathedral Street were Mackey's Seeds, followed by the Gresham Hotel, occupying four houses … then the Crown Hotel, then the Granville Hotel occupying three houses, then two houses acting as a temporary GPO, then the Hamman Hotel and Turkish Baths, then the fine Drogheda House, the right half of which had been rebuilt as the office of the Tramway Company.[9]

History was repeating itself. The Republicans, it seemed, had learnt nothing from the previous days. Again holed up in a heavily barricaded building, completely surrounded by superior forces, were some of the most experienced men of the IRA, waiting to be attacked. As at the Four Courts, there was no logistical plan in place and again no offensive action was taken.

Although urged by Cathal Brugha to revert to the guerrilla tactics that had been so successful against the British during the War of Independence, Traynor refused, fearing it would put more civilian lives at risk. He had sent dispatches to the brigades outside Dublin requesting relieving forces. His hope was that the Republican forces, who were numerically superior, would encircle the pro-Treaty forces, thus giving those in the city a fighting chance, or even enable them to clear a line of retreat. Seamus Robinson, O/C of the 3rd Tipperary Brigade, and now acting O/C of the 2nd Southern Division, was the only commandant to respond to Traynor's request. He sent a detachment of fully armed men, under the command of Mick Sheehan; it was, however, too little, too late.

Meanwhile, John A. Pinkman was posted in Amiens Street Station. He was part of a scouting party sent to search the surrounding area for Republican outposts. Night had fallen by this time and, as he recalled:

> There wasn't a soul abroad in the vicinity of Amiens Street ... and we felt a rare, uncanny quietness hanging over Dublin. We cut across the road in front of the station and then advanced very slowly down Amiens Street in extended order, keeping a tight grip on our rifles in case we were suddenly attacked ... our eyes searched the dark silent buildings for unclosed windows and doors left slightly ajar from which the muzzle of a rifle or a machine gun might suddenly emerge. It was almost midnight when we finally reached Mountjoy Square having scouted slowly and silently along the way which was supposed to be cleared of anti-Treatyites.[10]

Pinkman and his colleagues stayed in a house on Mountjoy Square for the night and managed to rest. Everyone knew that Sunday would bring more fighting, but for the present the city was quiet once more.

CHAPTER 11

SUNDAY 2 JULY

The pro-Treaty forces in the O'Connell Street area were under the command of Tom Ennis, O/C 2nd Eastern Division. He ordered his men to focus their efforts on removing the Republicans from the Block and the positions held by them in the area surrounding Parnell Square. Throughout the morning the firing continued, at times becoming increasingly intense.

The Lord Mayor of Dublin, Laurence O'Neill, and the Archbishop of Dublin, Dr Byrne, had tried but failed to broker a peace between the opposing sides, after which a full-scale assault was launched against the Republican strongholds. Thirty Republicans were taken prisoner in Harcourt Terrace, though the garrison in the Swan Hotel were firmly entrenched.

At Hughes and Moran's hotels, the pro-Treaty forces launched a full-scale attack. This area was under the command of Brigadier-General Paddy O'Daly, whose command post was in Amiens Street Station. The pro-Treaty forces were put in position on the Loop Line Bridge overlooking Lower Gardiner Street, from which heavy fire was concentrated on the Republicans. Seán Prendergast, who was in Hughes Hotel, stated:

The Treaty forces had brought up an armoured railway engine on which they had erected a trench mortar to pound at our positions. That engine and the railway itself afforded them very good cover, as well as the fact that they held undisputed use of the railway system … They had the protection of the gable ends of houses which met the bridge at that point. Our men were not so well fitted to counter that move – the only effective fire they could deliver was through a few loop-holes made in the walls of the corner house where only a few men could operate at any given time … In great extremity they were forced to abandon their positions and to fall back to other positions, having to vacate what, up to then, had been our main offensive and defensive flank positions.[1]

The garrison in Moran's were attacked at the same time, and communications between the two outposts were cut and could only be renewed during a lull in the fighting. In the meantime, the pro-Treaty forces had mounted an eighteen-pounder gun on the railway bridge and bombarded the hotels continuously; Moran's Hotel in particular bore the brunt of the assault. Inside the hotels, the men fought as best they could. Realising they were isolated, however, their thoughts turned inevitably to how long they could hold their position. Prendergast recalled:

As things stood then we were at a decided disadvantage in practically every way, the only thing in our favour being that while we held on, the Treaty forces might be delayed in making a grand assault on the garrison occupying portion of O'Connell Street [*sic*]. We must delay them as long as possible as a matter of principle. As the fight wore on the men held their nerve, they … behaved wonderfully cool, collected and determined, showing neither sign of hysteria or fuss, all under perfect control.[2]

The men continued to fight, but by the afternoon, with their firepower and ammunition drastically reduced, their thoughts turned to evacuation. In Hughes, it was decided to leave a token force behind to enable the main body of men to leave. Guns and other materials were hidden away and in all a garrison of fewer than twenty men remained. A similar decision was made to evacuate Moran's. Annie M. P. Smithson, who was in Moran's, stated that the garrison were to:

> … make our way – by tunnels which our engineers had made in the walls – higher up the street. But first there was the land-mine which our men had decided to let off the last thing before leaving the place … We, who were Red Cross workers, decided to remain until this was done; there might be someone hurt and perhaps left behind … At last, a rumble, increasing to a roar, and we knew the mine had gone off. The walls shook, we were almost covered with dust and whitewash – but, we were alive.[3]

Back at Hughes, there were now only twelve men left holding the building.[4] Having covered the safe evacuation of the main body of volunteers, the men could not continue to hold the building and surrendered. They were marched out, paraded in the streets and taken into the charge of the Dublin Guards, under Paddy O'Daly. They were then moved to Amiens Street Station and held there for two days, after which they were brought to Mountjoy Gaol, and later to Portobello Barracks.[5]

By the afternoon intense fighting had broken out in York Street and Aungier Street. At the Swan Hotel, the Republicans were coming under increasingly heavy fire. Almost directly opposite the Swan, the pro-Treaty forces had occupied Messrs

Fanagans, undertakers. This was as a result of Commandant Vinny Byrne, with two other soldiers, earlier driving unwittingly into the Republicans' line of fire. Byrne later stated:

> I didn't know the anti-Treaty forces had taken over the Swan Hotel at the corner of York Street, and they knocked the hell out of us. At the time I thought it was a street ambush and ordered my driver to go down Dick [Digges] Street round to Mercer Street, and we'd catch these fellows in York Street. We caught it again, from the houses this time.[6]

The battle went on for some time, and it was only when Paddy Griffin, National Army, arrived from Portobello Barracks in an armoured car, 'The Fighting Second', that the pro-Treaty forces were able to clear the area successfully.[7]

With this serious threat to the pro-Treaty forces now removed, attention turned to O'Connell Street and the remaining Republican outposts. Commandant Tom Ennis ordered that a cordon be thrown around these positions to isolate them, and by late afternoon the whole area came under heavy fire.

Back at the Block, the situation continued to deteriorate. Todd Andrews, during a lull in the firing, managed to make his way from his position in the Tramway Office to the headquarters section in the Hamman Hotel, where he found, among others, Oscar Traynor, Cathal Brugha, Éamon de Valera, Countess Markievicz, Art O'Connor and Austin Stack. Seán Dowling, also present, stated that, 'all except Brugha seemed at a loss as to what they should do, or even where they should be. Brugha was at no loss.'[8]

In the Gresham, Andrews had met Ernie O'Malley's brother,

Charlie. Soon afterwards, Charlie, while making his way into the lane behind the Gresham, was shot and killed by a National Army sniper. He was eighteen years old.

In the meantime, the pro-Treaty forces cordon was closing in. John A. Pinkman, in Amiens Street Station with ten other men, had been ordered to make their way back to Parnell Street to breach the Block. Their target was Bridgeman's tobacconists, on the corner of Parnell Street and O'Connell Street, which had been taken by the Republicans. This position was vital if the pro-Treaty forces were to make any headway in taking O'Connell Street. They cautiously made their way until they reached the crossroads at Parnell Street. On reaching their destination safely, they found Bridgeman's to be heavily barricaded. Having fired several volleys into the building, the party gained entry successfully, only to find it was deserted.

On further investigation at the rear of the premises the men discovered a hole 'big enough for a man to crawl through – which led into the next building'.[9] Pinkman and his colleagues searched the rest of the building. On arriving on the top floor he entered a corner room that overlooked the crossroads of Parnell Street and O'Connell Street. There he found what appeared to be a Republican sniper in position 'resting on some pillows with his rifle aimed out of the window and his fingers closed around the trigger'.[10]

Cautiously, Pinkman shouted to the man to surrender, but there was no reply; he was dead, having been shot through the head, most likely from one of the pro-Treaty armoured cars that were now converging on the area. Pinkman and his colleague discovered that this lone sniper had the whole area of the crossroads covered through a series of holes bored in the walls, giving him access to both Parnell Street and Cavendish Row. Having secured the building, the party regrouped and made their way through the series of buildings that had been tunnelled through. As Pinkman described it:

> It was a dangerous, nerve-wracking task as we searched for the hole in the wall that would lead into the next building. The holes had been made in the walls by the Irregulars who'd torn away the bricks until they'd made gaps large enough to permit them to crawl from one house to the next along the entire length of the block between Parnell Street and Findlater Place. As we made our way through the buildings we sometimes found ourselves being shot at from behind and realised we had bypassed the Irregulars. Sometimes we even fired in error at our own lads as we raced from room to room searching frantically for those holes torn in the brick work.[11]

Before the party had cleared the stronghold, they were ordered by their lieutenant to retreat to Bridgeman's. By then it was getting dark and the complex was unfamiliar to the pro-Treaty forces, so the Republicans now had the upper hand and could easily have attacked them.

Back at the Hamman, Traynor waited eagerly to find out whether his dispatch to the IRA outside Dublin had reached them. As stated earlier, Traynor's plan was to have the other brigades surround the pro-Treaty forces in Dublin. By this time, the Tipperary men, under Mick Sheehan, had reached Blessington. There to meet him was, among others, Ernie O'Malley, who, along with Seán Lemass, Joe Griffin, Tom Derrig and Paddy Rigney, had escaped from Jameson's Distillery after the surrender at the Four Courts. Determined to carry on the fight, they had made their way to Blessington and contacted the South Dublin Brigade and waited to receive orders to advance on Dublin. Lil O'Donnell, who had been in the Hamman, delivered a dispatch to O'Malley, who was waiting at Crooksling Barracks, from Traynor, 'in which he stated that he wanted rifles and ammunition forwarded first and then the men who would make their way unarmed to the Hamman Hotel'.[12] O'Malley, with his 150 men, reluctantly withdrew to Blessington.

CHAPTER 12

MONDAY 3 JULY

At about 2 a.m. on Monday, the pro-Treaty forces cautiously made their way through O'Connell Street in preparation for what was to be a full-scale attack on the Block and the last remaining Republican strongholds. By then, most of the city was in pro-Treaty hands and the cordon was drawing ever more tightly around the Republican positions centred in O'Connell Street and Parnell Square. The quiet of the night was shattered:

> ... when a vigorous attack on the position of the Irregulars was made by armoured cars and machine-gun lorries. One armoured car took up its position just outside the Metropole, another at the corner of Talbot Street, and a third on the other side of Nelson's Pillar. From here they poured in a rapid fire on the positions ... with machine guns and rifle grenades.[1]

Two machine guns placed in Arnott's Tower and Elvery's, respectively, were also used in the attack.

In Bridgeman's, Pinkman and his four colleagues were ordered again to search the maze of buildings for Republicans. Any they found were taken prisoner and held in Bridgeman's. At one point Pinkman and his colleagues came under heavy fire, to which they responded vigorously. They heard a woman shouting that she was a Red Cross nurse and to stop firing, which they did. On searching the woman, however, they found she was carrying a revolver, and she too was taken prisoner. They continued with their search until they eventually reached the end of the block at Findlater's store, where:

> we found ourselves on a first floor landing from which stairs led down to a store-room into which the Irregulars had retreated. The six or seven steps of the stairway led to another landing about four feet wide before a further six or seven steps led directly into the store-room at the bottom.[2]

Here, the Republicans had the advantage; they were in complete darkness in the storeroom and the pro-Treaty soldiers had to come to them. The soldiers were completely vulnerable as the light from the staircase made them clearly visible to the enemy lying in wait. Pinkman recalled:

> Each time we as much as put a foot on the stairs the Irregulars fired a volley up the stairs – and we knew we'd have to reach the landing below us before we would be in an effective firing position. We tried firing at them from every angle possible … but were unable to make any progress.[3]

After a few attempts, the party made their way down the stairs, firing as they went, but all the time coming under heavy fire. They finally made it safely to the doorway of the storeroom, which they found was barricaded. Eventually they gained entry but found:

it was so dark and silent that we had to light matches as we searched for the dead and wounded ... As we groped around the store-room we didn't find any Irregulars but one of our lads discovered a door which – to our surprise when we opened it – led directly into Findlater Place. We realised then that we'd finally driven the Irregulars right out of the block ... We dashed outside to search for them but Findlater Place was deserted.[4]

The whole row of buildings stretching from Bridgeman's to Findlater Place was now in the hands of the pro-Treaty forces. Opposite Bridgeman's, on the western corner of Parnell Street and O'Connell Street was the National Bank. It too had been taken by the Republicans, but was cleared successfully. With these two strategic buildings taken over, the pro-Treaty forces successfully severed the connection between the Block and the surrounding outposts at Barry's Hotel, 44 Parnell Square and the YMCA building, which was opposite the Block.

At 3.15 a.m. National Army headquarters released the following statement:

The Dublin Guard's enveloping movement in the O'Connell Street area is near completion. The Irregulars are now driven out of Earl Street, and their posts in Hickey's, Boyer's, Powell's and Nagle's are occupied by our Army. The Irregular's [sic] now only occupy that part of O'Connell Street stretching from the Tramways Company's offices to Findlater Place.

This block of buildings is now completely surrounded.

On the recapture of Bridgeman's, Parnell street [sic] 10 prisoners were taken, with their arms. One dead body was found on the premises.[5]

The city was once again quiet, but as the morning progressed, the fighting renewed, becoming more intense as the day wore on. The Block was being attacked aggressively, and inside the garrison did all they could to keep their spirits up. To try to lighten the mood, Linda Kearns, Muriel MacSwiney and Kathleen Barry, who were in the Hamman, took it upon themselves to make the men cocktails. Their good intentions failed miserably, though, so much so that one of the men suggested 'that they take it out to the Free Staters where it could prove lethal'.[6]

Meanwhile, in the Tramway Offices, Seán Dowling and his men were coming under increasingly heavy fire from the armoured cars and the troops in Elvery's and the La Scala Theatre, and the machine gunner in Arnott's Tower. It was during this encounter that Todd Andrews was wounded:

> I was returning the fire rather futilely with my rifle when a hail of bullets caught my firing slit, blasting sand from the barricades with great force into my forehead, right eye and cheek. A large bullet splinter penetrated my clothing, lodging in my forearm ... My arm was bleeding ... I was helped by Dowling to the first-aid station in the Gresham ... I was then removed by ambulance to the Mater Hospital.[7]

Throughout the day, the attack on the Block intensified. The Republican outposts were surrounded, and those in the Block were being hit from all directions: from the rear in Marlborough Street and from as many as five other positions on O'Connell Street and its side streets. Inside the Block, Traynor deliberated on what to do. His options were limited: either to try to evacuate the area and risk capture, or stay where they were and continue to fight against overwhelming odds, thus risking both the lives of his men and of ordinary citizens. Neither option was acceptable, but after some time he decided to evacuate the Block, leaving just a token force behind to cover their retreat. The leaders would attempt to make their way to the south side of the city, regroup and decide what their next course of action should be. The order to evacuate was given, and by some means word got through to the other outposts, including those in Barry's Hotel.

On receiving the order to evacuate, the garrison in Barry's hurriedly set about preparing the building. Annie Farrington was urged to leave the hotel, as it was going to be mined, but again she refused to leave her premises. She watched as the garrison set about laying mines all over the building, placing 'one under the front door and another under the roof in the top storey. They left guns sticking out the window when they were going.'[8]

Before they left, Miss Farrington asked one of the men to cut the lines connected to the mines, which he did, and the garrison quietly left the hotel. Farrington recalled:

William bolted all the doors and I went round all the rooms, switched on the lights and pulled in the guns – about a dozen of them – from the windows and stuck them up the chimney in the smoke-room. They were found by the Free State soldiers when they came.[9]

By 8 p.m. the firing had subsided to some degree. Back at the Gresham Hotel, Traynor and de Valera, together with seventy men and thirty women, left the hotel successfully, leaving Cathal Brugha in command of a token force of sixteen men. With Brugha were Art O'Connor, Dr Brennan, Nurse Linda Kearns, Muriel MacSwiney and Kathleen Barry. There was also a small detachment of men in the Hamman.

Some time after 9 p.m. the YMCA building in Upper O'Connell Street, which had been held by the Republicans, caught fire. The Fire Brigade were quickly on the scene and found the building heavily barricaded. The brigade attempted to subdue the fire from the front in O'Connell Street and at the rear in Moore Lane, but they were forced to abandon their efforts when the fighting between the pro-Treaty forces and Brugha's men in the Block resumed. Captain Myers of the Fire Brigade stated: 'The prolonged rifle and machine-gun fire grew very intense, and bullets became dangerously near … We had to take cover, and our attempts had only the effect of temporarily allaying the outbreak.'[10] It wasn't until the early hours of the morning, when the firing had died down, that the Fire Brigade were able to return and extinguish the blaze.

Hopelessly outnumbered and with very few weapons, Brugha and his men could not expect to hold out much longer, and the pro-Treaty forces expected a swift victory. This was not to be the case, however, and as Monday came to an end the pro-Treaty forces realised they would need much more than rifles and machine guns to remove the Republicans once and for all.

CHAPTER 13

TUESDAY 4 JULY

At 2 a.m. on Tuesday the pro-Treaty forces launched what they hoped would be their final assault on the Block. Three armoured cars in position at Nelson's Pillar led the assault. A reporter from *The Irish Times* noted:

> The gunners appeared to pick out particular objectives in the hotels, upon which they poured a withering fire, which was occasionally returned by the garrison. Machine guns were brought into operation, while smoke bombs and grenades were frequently hurled by the attackers.[1]

Back at Bridgeman's, John A. Pinkman and a Lewis gunner were ordered to occupy the top floor of the building. They placed their gun at a window, from which they were able to cover the west side of O'Connell Street. As the morning wore on, the men became bored and, while watching the street for Republican activity, they noticed the YMCA sign on the building opposite and the two men began to compete to knock the lettering off the building with the Lewis gun. They then decided to use a small window near the top of the YMCA building as a target. Shortly afterwards, the men noticed some smoke around the area they had been shooting at and, thinking they might have hit a gas pipe, Pinkman decided the best thing to do was to shoot a whole drum of ammunition into the window. He recalled:

> I fired the entire drum into the window. Jasus! All of a sudden clouds of smoke – followed by tongues of flame – billowed out of the window.
>
> We quickly pulled the Lewis gun away from the window sill … The two of us agreed not to tell anyone we caused the fire, but that we should send word to those of our lads whom we knew were in Moore Street to be on the lookout for any Irregulars trying to escape from the rear of Upper Sackville [O'Connell] Street.[2]

They managed to get word to their colleagues, after which a party of troops made their way through a series of buildings to reach the YMCA, where there were Republicans who were trying to evacuate the building as a result of the fire. Three soldiers found themselves in Moore Lane at the rear of the building, and then became trapped when the back door of the house they had come through slammed shut. Their only hope of escape was to retreat along the alley to Parnell Street, but they were seen by a woman, who alerted the Republicans in the YMCA. The soldiers were fired on, and two were wounded, but they managed to get away and the Republicans in the YMCA soon surrendered. All attention was now focused on the Block.

Inside the Gresham, the small garrison fought on. The hospital, which had originally been situated in the billiard room in the Hamman, had been moved to the Granville Hotel, as the Hamman was coming under heavy fire. Linda Kearns continued with her work of tending the wounded with the help of Muriel MacSwiney and Kathleen Barry.

The firing continued throughout the day. Republican snipers had taken up positions to distract the pro-Treaty forces. They were in place at Eden Quay in Messrs Mooney's and on neighbouring rooftops opposite the Ballast Office, which was held by the pro-Treaty forces. At one point in the attack, the pro-Treaty forces made their way close to the Block in an armoured car, so close that they were able to throw explosives through the ground floor windows of the hotels. Despite what seemed to be an airtight cordon around the Block, Seán M. Glynn managed to get through to the Gresham and convey a message from Oscar Traynor to Brugha that reinforcements were not coming and surrender was the safest option. Brugha refused.

At 6 p.m. another sustained attack was launched on the Block. Pinkman and his colleague had been repositioned in Findlater's, and were entrenched on an upper floor, where they could cover the whole of Findlater Place and Thomas Lane, at the rear of the Block. Their aim was to cover the rear of the buildings in Thomas Lane and to watch for any Republicans attempting to evacuate. With their Lewis gun at the ready, they waited.

Back in O'Connell Street, a duel was taking place between a sniper in the Hamman and a pro-Treaty soldier at Nelson's Pillar. The soldier was backed up by machine-gun fire and soon enough a white flag was carried from the Hamman, and a group of men, fifteen in all, surrendered and were taken into custody.

Simultaneously, at St Thomas's church, near Findlater Place, another white flag was seen. The firing stopped 'and about thirty men marched out and surrendered. They were quickly surrounded and disarmed, and … were marched away under a heavy escort to Amiens Street Station.'[3]

The pro-Treaty forces then focused on the last remaining Republican stronghold – the Gresham Hotel. In an advance movement, some soldiers lay on the ground in O'Connell Street, while the remaining troops advanced in open formation towards the Gresham, but were forced to retreat after one soldier was wounded.

At 8 p.m. the final assault began. Heavy firing from rifle grenades and bombs were concentrated on the Gresham. At 9 p.m. one of the eighteen-pounders was put into position at the corner of Henry Street and O'Connell Street, and once again the sound of the booming gun echoed over the city. The Republicans remained determined to resist the attack and maintained a continuous fire on the pro-Treaty force's positions.

The eighteen-pounder was positioned behind two Lancia armoured lorries, between which the muzzle of the gun protruded, aiming at the Block. But even with all this protection, the soldiers were not safe. A sniper in the Block managed to shoot a soldier in the head, but amazingly he was not seriously wounded.[4] The attack continued until about 10.15 p.m., after which the firing began to die down. During this time, citizens were emerging onto the streets, trying to catch a glimpse of the last stand by the Republicans, regardless of the danger to themselves. Unfortunately, a number of people were wounded by sniper fire.

Between 11 p.m. and midnight the thunderous sounds of guns blasting away and bombs exploding were heard, and then the attack suddenly stopped, but everyone knew it would not be long before the guns would be put into action once more. And so another day ended, just as before, with both sides still holding on with fierce determination. Observers could only wonder what Wednesday would bring.

CHAPTER 14

WEDNESDAY 5 JULY

Wednesday morning began with the sound of gunfire echoing around the city, but this time it was the field gun blasting away at the Block. From its position at the corner of Henry Street, the gun's sights were trained on the Hamman and the Tramway Office. Believing that there might still be Republicans in those buildings, the pro-Treaty forces kept up a constant attack, firing the eighteen-pounder gun throughout the night, the shells pounding the façade of the buildings. This barrage was kept up until 8 a.m., when the firing suddenly stopped and, when the dust and smoke had settled, the damage inflicted on the Block was clearly visible. Breaches had been made in the wall of the Hamman, but the building was completely empty. At the Gresham, the occasional shot from a sniper could still be heard. At one point a soldier at the field gun was slightly wounded in the leg by sniper fire. It was clear that Brugha and his men were not going to give up; if the Gresham was to be taken, the pro-Treaty forces would have to go and take it from them.

A reporter from *The Irish Times*, who was with the soldiers in the Sackville Street Club, opposite the Block, bore witness to the final attack on the stronghold:

In every house lay the litter of the combat, such as empty cartridge cases, live cartridge cases which had jammed in a Lewis gun, rifles fitted with auxiliary caps for firing No. 5 Mills bombs ... There were tired soldiers taking a hasty rest or brewing a cup of tea.

All the houses had suffered considerably from rifle and machine-gun fire:

I was directly opposite the battered Hamman, and at 11.30 saw approaching the armoured lorries which made the first attempt. Into one of the breaches they flung about a dozen bombs ... A few minutes later a more successful attempt was made.

Another minute and the unused rifle cartridges began to explode with the heat, one by one at first, and then in continuous succession as if two or three machine-guns were firing from the building.[1]

Fire had by then broken out in the Hamman, and spread quickly to neighbouring buildings. Soon the Hamman was a mass of flames and the danger was immense to both the Republicans and National Army soldiers alike, because the ammunition stored by the Republicans was now exploding in the fire, but still the battle raged on.

The Fire Brigade were soon on hand to try to quell the blaze, but they had an enormous battle ahead of them. All sections of the brigade turned out, with those from Tara Street fire station dealing with the fire from a position in Thomas Lane at the rear of the Block. The men from Thomas Street station, on the south side of the city attacked the fire head-on in O'Connell Street, and the other two sections, from Buckingham Street and Dorset Street, were in position at Findlater Place. The firemen gave no thought to their own safety as the battle continued around them while they worked to control the blaze. However, the fighting became so intense at one point that the men were ordered to fall back,[2] and despite all their efforts the Hamman could not be saved. The fire had spread so rapidly that within a short time the building had begun to collapse; and neighbouring buildings soon suffered the same fate. Amid this chaos the battle continued.

About 12.40 p.m. a man was seen on the roof of the Gresham. Waving a white flag, he shouted to the soldiers down on the street below. Assuming that this was a sign of surrender, a party of troops made their way to J. W. Mackey's premises, next to the Gresham, and attempted to gain entry. Some of the troops succeeded in getting into Mackey's and were able to reach a breach in the wall on the first floor leading into the Gresham. Meanwhile, three other soldiers attacked the front door of the Gresham vigorously with rifle butts and hammers, until suddenly a number of shots burst through the door, forcing the soldiers to retreat. The other soldiers were also forced to retreat, having come under heavy fire. Outside the hotel, Captain Dan Stapleton was sitting in an armoured car. He was shot in the neck by one of the men in the Gresham, but miraculously he survived.

At this time the Republicans had no intention of surrendering. The man who had waved the flag had done so to warn the troops of the mines that had been placed in the building. By some means, Seán M. Glynn, who had earlier brought Traynor's message to Brugha to surrender, managed to return to the Gresham with yet another message from Traynor: reinforcements were not coming and Brugha was to surrender immediately. Again, he refused. Glynn, while attempting to leave the Gresham for the second time, was wounded and taken to the Mater Hospital.

With the buildings crashing down around him, and in what was now becoming an untenable position, Brugha's determination remained steadfast, just as it had during the Easter Rising when, despite being severely wounded, he had held back the advancing British forces in the South Dublin Union: 'He remained undaunted, comforting the wounded, encouraging the defenders, never allowing his own nerve to slacken for a moment ...'[3] However, under the fierce attack that was being levelled against them, the small garrison would not be able to hold out for much longer.

The armoured cars took it in turns to pour streams of bullets into the Gresham. When the gun of one car became too hot to continue firing, the car moved off and another took its place, continuing to fire with deadly accuracy; by 2.30 p.m. the Gresham itself was alight. Garry Holohan, brother of Commandant Paddy Holohan, was in the Gresham just before it caught fire. With four men he attempted to escape, but they ran into a party of troops and, with no other option, they surrendered and were taken into the care of Commandant McGuinness, National Army. Some of the men were wounded, but they did not appear downhearted, despite what they had been through: 'They seemed to be all in good spirits and were smoking cigarettes – a supply of which was offered by their captors.'[4]

With the Gresham now a raging inferno, ammunition in the

building exploded and by 3 p.m. the shooting had stopped almost completely. The soldiers watched as the hotel was consumed by fire. But the battle was not yet over. Brugha and his small detachment retreated to the Granville Hotel, the last tenable position in the Block and prepared to make their last stand.

The fight resumed once again, but this time, determined to end the battle once and for all, the eighteen-pounder gun was called into action again. It pounded shell after shell into the Granville, continuing for some time. Eventually some soldiers were able to make their way up O'Connell Street and succeeded in gaining entry to the building. While doing this, however, they were fired on by the garrison, some of whom were in the entrance hall of the hotel. One soldier was wounded.

The Granville, which had been the hospital since Tuesday, had a Red Cross flag flying over it and as a result it had not been targeted deliberately. This no longer mattered to the National Army, and an order to attack was given, after which, 'the gun in Henry Street opened up and threw four or five dozen shells into the building, while an armoured car let loose a sustained fire on the building'.[5]

By 5 p.m. the Granville Hotel, the last bastion of the Republicans, was on fire. Not wanting to risk the lives of his men, Cathal Brugha finally ordered his small garrison to surrender. At first the men refused to leave, but after some persuasion they relented. Moira Kennedy O'Byrne, who was in the Granville at the time, recalled:

As we were marching out I passed through what had been the Turkish Baths and saw Cathal Brugha kneeling on a mat and

confessing to one of the friars. I shall never forget that sight. It
was his last confession.[6]

At around 7 p.m., and with the Granville completely consumed
by fire, the roof collapsed. Soon afterwards, shouts of 'Surrender' were heard. A white flag emerged in Thomas Lane at the
rear of the Granville. Waving the flag, Art O'Connor led out
his small party of Volunteers, about twenty in all, together with
Muriel MacSwiney and Kathleen Barry. The group was quickly
surrounded and taken into custody, but Cathal Brugha was
nowhere to be found. Many feared he had been caught in the
blaze. In fact, he had chosen to remain in the building, and with
him stayed Dr Brennan and Nurse Linda Kearns.

The Fire Brigade quickly made their way to Thomas Lane
and tried to gain entry into the Granville by the rear exit doors.
As they broke down the doors there suddenly appeared 'a low-
sized, smoke-stained man [who] rushed out with revolver
drawn'.[7]

In an effort to escape, Brugha made his way down Thomas
Lane, running towards a party of troops. He was called on to
halt but refused. A volley of shots rang out, but one bullet was
all it took; Cathal Brugha fell to the ground, mortally wounded.
Nurse Linda Kearns and Dr Brennan ran to his assistance, but
his femoral artery had been severed. Brugha was rushed by
ambulance to the Mater Hospital and Linda Kearns stayed with
him, holding the severed artery between her fingers. With that
volley of shots in Thomas Lane, the battle for Dublin ended.

CHAPTER 15

AFTERMATH

On Thursday 6 July, the people woke to the eerie calm that had descended over the city. Gone was the sound of the field guns. As the people ventured onto the streets, they saw their city in ruins. In the course of the eight days of fighting, eighty buildings had been either completely or partially destroyed across the city.

Later that day, the government issued a national call to arms, having granted permission for an additional 20,000 troops to be raised for the National Army. The government realised that the Civil War was not going to end with the fall of Dublin. Service in the army would be for six months or for the duration of the conflict. Unlike the situation when recruiting first began, this time the call to arms was advertised to the masses.

The funerals of six soldiers of the National Army who had been killed during the fighting also took place on 6 July. The dead soldiers were Captain Luke Condron, Sergeants Patrick Lowe and Richard Reid, and Privates Thomas Hogan, Patrick McGarry and Patrick Walsh. The funeral procession started from City Hall and made its way to Glasnevin Cemetery via O'Connell Street.

Luke Condron's body was removed from Arran Quay church,

where it had remained overnight. The coffin was mounted on a gun-carriage and drawn by four horses.[1] The National Army's pipers' band led the funeral cortège as it proceeded slowly down Arran Quay to Grattan Bridge. At the same time, the remains of Sergeant Lowe and Private McGarry were removed from the Mater Hospital, and the remains of Sergeant Reid and Privates Hogan and Walsh were removed from Jervis Street Hospital and proceeded to Capel Street. Each coffin was draped in the Tricolour and the coffins were placed on hearses, each drawn by four horses. These hearses joined the funeral procession of Captain Condron and continued their journey surrounded by soldiers of the Dublin Guard with arms reversed.

The cortège then made its way up Parliament Street and around into O'Connell Street. Amid the smouldering ruins, the procession slowly made its way through the city as thousands of people lined the route to pay their respects. A short mass was held in the Glasnevin Cemetery church, and the six men were interred in the National Plot in Glasnevin, after which the 'Last Post' was sounded and three volleys were fired over the grave.[2]

On Friday 7 July, in response to the government's call to arms, throngs of men turned out to join the army. Among those eager to join were men who had fought in the First World War, but most joined out of necessity. The government had not expected such a response and, to cope with demand, five recruiting depots were set up across the city.

That morning the people learned that Cathal Brugha was dead. After he was taken to the Mater Hospital on Wednesday evening, he underwent an operation and had shown signs of recovery. However, by Friday his condition had deteriorated and he succumbed to his injuries at 10.45 a.m. According to the coroner, 'death was due to shock and haemorrhage following a bullet wound'.[3] Cathal Brugha, hero of the Easter Rising and the War of Independence, was gone. He was forty-eight years old. The Republicans had suffered their first major casualty, and many more would follow.

Because of the situation, it was impossible for the IRA to perform the funeral, so that honour fell to the members of Cumann na mBan. Bridget O'Mullane recalled:

> I then got an order to get my uniform and report to Tara Hall. On going there I was told I was to act as one of the Guard of Honour to the body of Cathal Brugha … When four of us Cumann na mBan arrived in uniform late that night at the Mater Hospital, we were told by the Sister-in-Charge that we could not be allowed to act as guard during the night, but the Reverend Mother promised that we would be admitted as early as we liked the following morning … We made no fuss but went home and returned early next morning to take up duty at the bier of Cathal Brugha. We and other members of Cumann na mBan marched in his funeral procession and only came off duty when he was buried.[4]

Cathal Brugha was interred in the Republican Plot in Glasnevin Cemetery on Monday 10 July. As with the funerals of the soldiers, crowds again lined the route. Unfortunately, this was a scene that would be repeated all over the country as the war dragged on.

Another loss suffered by the Republicans was the death of Paddy O'Brien, O/C of the Four Courts garrison. Despite being wounded, he had refused to go to hospital and was taken to his home. Though in immense pain he refused to stay out of the fight, and eventually made his way to Blessington, where he met Ernie O'Malley. Their aim was to go to Enniscorthy with the men from Blessington and remove the pro-Treaty forces based there. In the ensuing fight, O'Brien was shot in the lung and succumbed to his wounds on 11 July. His remains were taken back to Dublin and he was buried quite close to Brugha in the Republican Plot in Glasnevin Cemetery.[5]

CHAPTER 16

CONCLUSION

When the first shell hit the Four Courts on the morning of 28 June, it did not just mark the beginning of the Irish Civil War, it also ended the hope of any Republican victory. For months, both sides had done all they could to avoid the inevitable conflict, but when it did come, the Republicans were the least prepared. The divisions in the Republican side were mainly responsible for this failure. Had they taken the initiative in the months immediately after the split, the outcome might have been different. After all, they were numerically stronger, their men were mainly experienced veterans of the Easter Rising and the War of Independence, and, very importantly, their men were loyal.

However, the divisions within the Republican movement prevented any offensive action being taken. Cathal Brugha and Liam Lynch believed wholeheartedly in the Republic, but also believed that the will of the people, who had suffered so much in the preceding years, was the most important thing. Both did all in their power to avert civil war, but their efforts proved futile with the setting up of the Executive. Once the Executive broke away from the main Republican body, Lynch had no control over these men, and thus any chance of cohesive planning was impossible.

The members of the Executive themselves, though claiming to represent the majority of opinion among the Republicans, failed to show any real qualities of leadership. This can be seen from the takeover of the Four Courts, when they refused time and again to act in a decisive manner, despite being urged by many of their junior officers to do so. They believed, somewhat naïvely, that the IRA would unite and once again fight the common enemy. The blame for this failure to act can rest only with the members of the Executive in the Four Courts – that is Liam Mellows, Rory O'Connor and others. Ben Doyle best summed up the situation when he stated that, 'the whole thing was taken in a half-hearted slipshod manner'.[1] This wait-and-see attitude of the Executive continued throughout the attack on the Four Courts.

There was then the impossible position in which Paddy O'Brien found himself. As O/C of the Four Courts, the Executive should have answered to him. He should have been allowed to conduct the battle in whatever way he saw fit, but at every point he was overruled by the Executive. Even though they were under his overall command, they blocked his every decision, as Peadar O'Donnell noted:

Paddy O'Brien was OC in the Four Courts, a very promising lad. It was his misfortune that the Executive of the IRA was in the same building. That undermined his authority; he could not prepare its defence properly, and when the attack came he could not undertake the break-out actions he would have liked to take. The result was that after three days, 180 of us were taken prisoner, and all but five who escaped, ended up in Mountjoy shortly afterwards.[2]

The pro-Treaty side was also not free from division, and was just as naïve in its actions as the Republicans. On the one hand there was Arthur Griffith and other members of the government who believed that civil war was inevitable, and the best thing to do would be to act quickly and end it as soon as possible. Then there were the military men – Michael Collins and Richard Mulcahy – who saw that they were in no real position to initiate a fight, and if they did act against the Republicans too early, it could be their undoing. They knew that the army was weak in terms of fighting men, and that if they made the first move they could be surrounded by the Southern Divisions and defeated; they had to act cautiously. Additionally, they could not even depend on the loyalty of their men. Seán Lemass, Paddy O'Brien, Dinny O'Brien and Simon Donnelly, to name just a few, had all been in Beggars Bush Barracks after the British evacuated. Once the IRA Convention was prohibited by the government in March, they all left the army and openly declared their loyalty to the Republic. The mutinies and desertions continued right up to the attack on the Four Courts.

Once the split among the Republicans had appeared after the June Convention, Collins and Mulcahy saw their opportunity. They hoped to be able to reason with Liam Lynch, to avoid his being drawn into the conflict and thus keeping the south neutral. In this way, Collins and Mulcahy hoped to isolate the Executive in the Four Courts and have the chance to limit the fighting to Dublin. However, Collins' only real hope of appeasing Lynch was with the constitution, which would have to be Republican in nearly all its content, but this was never going to be allowed by the British Government, who would see it as undermining the Treaty; something they would not tolerate. Collins and Mulcahy were also naïve in thinking that once the fight did start, the Republicans would not reunite. It was this thinking that led Mulcahy to order the release of Liam Lynch and his men after their arrest on 28 June – a fatal mistake on Mulcahy's part.

Though the Republicans did reunite, their lack of planning thwarted their every move. While the Executive had their headquarters in the Four Courts, Oscar Traynor had set up his headquarters in Barry's Hotel. But as in the courts, there was no cohesive strategy. Traynor ordered the seizure of buildings on the east side of Upper O'Connell Street, which offered no direct link to the Four Courts. Once the pro-Treaty forces got into position on the west side of O'Connell Street any hope that Traynor had of sending reinforcements to the courts was to prove futile.

This lack of foresight continued even when the pro-Treaty forces were bombarding the Block. Ernie O'Malley had more than 100 men ready to march on Dublin from Blessington, but at the last moment they were ordered by Traynor to fall back. The pro-Treaty forces at that time were stretched to the limit and were not in a position to mount an offensive attack against this contingent, as Peadar O'Donnell noted:

> Paddy Daly [sic], who had led the attack on the Four Courts, told me that he had not the slightest hope that he could reach it [Blessington], had he been opposed. Instead we made soldiers of the Free State Army by putting up a show of a fight while retreating away from them.[3]

Possibly the most controversial aspect of the fighting in Dublin was the destruction of the Four Courts. Over the years there has been much debate as to whether the records office, which, as noted earlier, housed priceless historical documents dating back centuries, and the central hall in the courts were deliberately blown up by the Republicans, or whether it was the shelling by pro-Treaty forces that caused a fire resulting in the exploding of the mines that had been laid throughout the building. Having looked at many sources to find out the true cause of the explosions, it is not possible to say for certain that it was an act deliberately committed by the Republicans, or that it was unfortunate collateral damage. Both sides emphatically denied that they were responsible for the explosions, so in order to address this issue, the evidence from both sides needs to be examined.

The Republicans had indeed mined the courts. The orderlies section, based in the records office, was packed with explosives and other incendiary materials. When the attack came, Paddy O'Brien was prepared to destroy the building; he sent Ned Kelleher to evacuate the orderlies and oversee the destruction of the building, but Kelleher was arrested before he could reach the records office, which was then in the hands of the pro-Treaty forces. According to Simon Donnelly, it was the fire caused by the shelling of the Four Courts that triggered the first explosion.[4]

With regard to the second explosion, in the central hall, there are again conflicting accounts. Here too, O'Brien was prepared to blow some of the mines, hoping to create a breach to enable them to escape, but Rory O'Connor refused to allow him to do this. From the start, the Executive showed an unwillingness to act in an offensive way; they refused to leave the Four Courts when they had the chance, again at the request of O'Brien, as they believed that such a move would be tantamount to abandoning the Republic. O'Connor had given his word that no harm would come to the archives – a noble statement under the circumstances. It is quite hard to see that, after all that time, and having overruled O'Brien every time he wanted to make a proactive decision, that at this point, with the end in sight, the Executive would make a decision to blow up the building when all along they had not taken the initiative and only reacted to events. There is one more possibility, which is that a lone volunteer caused the explosion. This is quite plausible because, as has been seen, there were many in the Four Courts who were eager for action. However, to date no proof of this has been found.

On the pro-Treaty side, there is the issue of the shells used to attack the courts. The pro-Treaty forces themselves stated that no incendiary shells were used in the assault. But on 29 June they had received a large amount of high-explosive British shells that had been shipped from Carrickfergus. There were also four eighteen-pounder guns trained on the Four Courts, though one gun was held back in reserve. From one gun alone, 375 shells were fired at the Four Courts at the command of Captain Johnny Doyle.[5] Considering that this number of shells was fired from just *one* gun, if the other eighteen-pounders are also taken into consideration (though not knowing how many shells they fired), it is quite possible that the explosion was indeed caused by a fire as a result of the Four Courts being bombarded from all sides.

As stated by Simon Donnelly, pro-Treaty forces used incendiary bombs.[6] This was corroborated by Volunteer Brogan of the National Army, who said in an interview with Ernie O'Malley that James Brennan was firing incendiary grenades at the Republicans from the records office after the building had been taken by the pro-Treaty forces.[7] Also, Paddy O'Daly, having alerted the Fire Brigade that the courts were on fire, refused to call a ceasefire to allow them to tackle the blaze, which despite meaning the difference of only a few minutes, enabled the fire to spread quickly, reaching the records office and possibly causing the explosion. However, this is all conjecture, and if the answer to the question of what actually caused the explosions is to be answered definitively, further investigation is needed.

What is certain is that, after eight days of fighting, Dublin city was devastated. Among the combatants on both sides, casualties were relatively low. At least twenty-eight combatants from both sides were killed in the fighting or died as a result of their injuries. The pro-Treaty forces suffered more in terms of soldiers wounded, most of these because of the explosions in the Four Courts. But as during the previous conflict, the ordinary people of Dublin suffered the most throughout the battle. Not only was their everyday life disrupted, but in terms of casualties it was the citizens who paid the price for a conflict they did not ask for or want any part in. When the fighting ended in Dublin, the total known casualties were sixty-one killed and 274 wounded, mainly civilians.

As Dublin city lay in ruins, the National Army, with its new recruits, went to war once again. The battle for Dublin had lasted eight days; the Civil War was to last eleven months. The effects of both were felt for generations, and are still felt to this day, be it politically, historically or socially. But as the centenary of the Civil War draws nearer, the futility and ultimately the tragedy of those eight days of fighting in Dublin can be seen in Glasnevin Cemetery. Among others in the Republican Plot lie Cathal Brugha, Paddy O'Brien, Rory O'Connor and Peadar Breslin. A short distance away in the National Army Plot lie the remains of Luke Condron, Dan Brennan, Thomas Mandeville and Patrick Lowe, with others, all of whom lost their lives in the Civil War. They are all buried in the same cemetery, in the same city, in the same country, and the question still remains, as important today as it was in 1922: what was it all for?

Appendix 1

Republican Constitution

Oglaigh Na h-Eireann

Draft Constitution and Rules

1. The Army shall be known as the Irish Republican Army.
2. It shall be on a purely Volunteer Army basis.

Objects

3. Its objects shall be:

    - To guard the honour and maintain the independence of the Irish Republic.

    - To protect the rights and liberties common to the people of Ireland.

    - To place its services at the disposal of an established Republican Government which faithfully upholds the above objects.

Control of the Army

4. The Army shall be controlled by an Executive of sixteen which shall be appointed by a Committee of twenty-five elected as follows:

    - Each Province elects five delegates.

    - Each Province nominates five further delegates from whom the whole Convention will elect the remaining five. Any serving Volunteer to be eligible to act on the Executive. This Executive shall have supreme control of the Army, and the Executive shall not itself, directly or indirectly, be subordinate to, or controlled by any other body: Subject to any alterations necessary to put into operation section 3 (Sub-Section C) above. Such proposed alterations to be sanctioned by a General Convention.

Duties and Power of Executive

5. The duties of the Executive shall be to define policy for the Army. It shall have supreme control over the Army Council and General Headquarters Staff. It shall not, however, have power to interfere with General Headquarters Staff in respect of purely Army matters, such as Organisation, Training, method of conducting operations, etc. Ten shall form a quorum at Meetings of the Executive.

Financial Powers

6. The Executive shall be responsible for the raising and safeguarding of funds for Army purposes.

Executive Meetings

7. The Executive shall meet at least every two months. In the event of a vacancy occurring on the Executive it shall be filled by co-option.

Army Council

8. The Executive shall appoint an Army Council of seven of which four shall be chosen from the members of Executive, and the remaining three may be appointed from outside the Executive. Four shall form a quorum at meetings of the Army Council. In the event of a vacancy occurring on the Council it shall be filled by co-option, to be approved by the Executive.

General Headquarters Staff

9. The Executive will appoint a Chief of Staff, who will appoint his Staff.

DUTIES OF ARMY COUNCIL

10. The Army Council shall carry out the functions of the Executive when the latter is not in session, but the Executive alone shall have power to declare Peace or War; such declaration must be supported by at least ten votes. A meeting of the Executive shall be called, if requested by two members of the Army Council, or three members of the Executive.

GENERAL CONVENTION

11. A General Convention representative of the whole Army shall meet at least once in each twelve months, and shall elect a Committee to appoint an Executive as in Section 4, who shall hold office until the next General Convention. It shall also receive a report from the Chief of Staff, and a financial statement from the Executive.

SYSTEM OF REPRESENTATION

12. The system of representation shall be as follows:
    - At a Company parade called for the purpose, one delegate shall be elected to attend a Brigade Convention where the number of men on parade does not exceed thirty men; two delegates where the number of men is over thirty and under seventy-one; three delegates where the number on parade exceeds seventy men; and an additional delegate for every thirty men over 100.
    - The election shall be held by ballot.

BRIGADE CONVENTION

13. The Constitution of the Brigade Convention shall be as follows:
    - The Brigade Commandant and two members of his Staff as elected by the Staff.
    - Each Battalion Commandant and one member of his Staff elected by the Staff.

- The Company delegates as elected in accordance with the instructions detailed above.
- The Staff in this connection shall be taken as including the Officers commanding Special Services.

14. The Brigade Convention shall elect delegates to represent the Brigade at the General Convention. The number of delegates to be so elected shall be 5% of the total number of delegates present at the Brigade Convention. In the event of such percentage resulting in a whole number and a fraction, the nearest whole number will be the number of delegates. The individual delegates so chosen need not necessarily be selected from those present at the Convention, but must be active members of the Brigade or of the Staff of the Division to which the Brigade is attached.

GENERAL CONVENTION

15. The constitution of the General Convention shall be as follows:
    - All members of the Executive.
    - All members of the Army Council.
    - All members of the General Headquarters Staff.
    - All Divisional Commandants, and two other members of the Divisional Staff as elected by that Staff.
    - The delegates selected at the Brigade Convention.

VOTING AT CONVENTION

16. Voting on Motions shall be carried out as decided by the Chairman of the Convention.

17. The Chairman of the General Convention shall be chosen by the Convention.

QUORUM

18. The number to form a quorum at a General Convention shall be two-thirds of

the total number of delegates entitled to attend.

EXTRAORDINARY CONVENTION

19. An Extraordinary Convention shall be called if required:

- By a two-thirds majority of the Executive.
- By a two-thirds majority of GHQ.
- By a two-thirds majority of the Divisional Commandants, provided they represent two-thirds the total strength of the whole Army.

MEMBERSHIP OF ARMY

20. Only such persons shall be allowed to remain in, or shall be admitted to the Army who take the Oath of Allegiance to the Irish Republic. No person holding any rank in any other Army shall be enrolled in the Irish Republican Army.

OATH

21. The Oath of Allegiance to be taken by every member of the Army shall be as follows:

- I ...., do solemnly swear that to the best of my knowledge and ability I will support and defend the Irish Republic against all enemies foreign and domestic that I will bear true faith and allegiance to the same. I do further swear that I do not, and shall not, yield a voluntary support to any pretended Government, Authority, or Power within Ireland hostile or inimical to that Republic. I take this obligation freely without any reservation or purpose of evasion so help me God.

AMENDING OF CONSTITUTION

22. It shall require a majority of two-thirds of the General Convention to amend any Article of the Constitution.

Source: Military Archives

APPENDIX 2

MEMBERS OF THE FOUR COURTS GARRISON 1922

No. 1 Section

Lieutenant Joseph McHenry
Sergeant William Gannon
Thomas 'Skinner' O'Reilly
John Cullinane
Henry Robinson
John Rooney
Francis Kelly
Patrick Byrne
Louis Lambe
Thomas Keenan
John Wickham
Charles Oliver
J. J. Kavanagh
Joseph Page
Martin Forsyth
Joseph Kavanagh
James Keogh

William Brennan
James Farrington
Thomas Ryan
Terence Byrne
Patrick Smyth
Dennis Brennan
Sergeant Cook Patrick McBride
Chris White
Anthony O'Moore
John McDermot
Martin Moloney
Tom Maloney
Charles Cullen
William Bannon
William Dowdall
Thomas Brady
Vincent Lalor

No. 2 Section

Lieutenant Frank Cotter
Matthew Lacey
Cathal 'Chummy' Hogan
Seán Brunswick
John J. Cunningham

Daniel Kane
John McGoldrick
Daniel Seery
Patrick McHenry
Mick Kavanagh

John Kelly
— McCann
Thomas Scanlon
John Saunders
Patrick McGrowder
Hugh Early
Daniel O'Connell
James Connaghty
Andrew O'Reilly
Joseph O'Connor

Dave Murphy
Mick Griffin
Dan Connolly
— McCallig
Jim Scully
Jack Brady
Patrick Farrell
Peter Dolan
John Kelleher

No. 3 Section

Lieutenant Seán Burke
Sergeant Patrick Morrissey
— Killeen
Chris Reid
Edward Gahan
John Delaney
Johnny McDonald
Patrick Mooney
Patrick Moore
Joseph Swan
John Mahon
Patrick Russell
Eamonn Moore
Michael Kelly
Thomas O'Brien
Charles Clarke
Patrick McSweeney

Patrick Buckley
James Fox
Chris Shortall
Charlie McGowan
Charles Hayden
Shaun Nolan
Billy Donohue
John McQuaid
— Stanley
Dick Toban
Jimmy O'Hanlon
John Black
Edward O'Brien
Matt Kelly
Jack Cunningham
Mick McCabe

No. 4 Section

Lieutenant Brian Leahy
John Nugent
Joseph Nugent
Joseph Murphy
James McVeigh
Frank Martin
John Martin
John O'Neill
Michael Delaney
John Salinger
Lawrence Nelson
Michael McAteer
Francis Kavanagh
Andrew Minto
John Brennan
William Irons
Paddy Byrne
John Corcoran

James Tutty
— Tracey (Armoured Car Driver)
William Moran
Dan McArt
Dan Kane
Donald O'Reilly
Michael Creegan
Paddy Corrigan
Liam Kavanagh
Paddy O'Moore
Jim Curry
Vincent Burke
Paddy Long
— Cunningham
Patrick Cleary
Patrick Durnim

No. 5 Section

Sergeant Thomas Morrissy
David Ritchie
John Pidgeon
John Nugent
Patrick Nevin
Paddy Flynn
John Wosser
James O'Connor
John Mullens
Thomas Wall

Seán Cusack
Joseph Valentine
Gerard Morrissey
Frank McMahon
Gus Ryan
Thomas Loughry
Edward Harris
Michael Keogh
Andrew Jones
Christopher Coleman

Red Cross Section

Lieutenant Vincent Gogan
Michael Kelly
Chris Hughes

Steve Gogan
Fred Martin

MEMBERS OF FOUR COURTS EXECUTIVE, OFFICERS AND OTHER RANK AND FILE VOLUNTEERS

Rory O'Connor
Liam Mellows
Joseph McKelvey
Ernie O'Malley
Commandant Paddy O'Brien
Tom Derrig
Joseph Griffin
Peadar O'Donnell
Richard Barrett
Seán Lemass
Simon Donnelly
Seán MacBride
Lieutenant Matthew 'Mattie' McDonnell
Lieutenant Police Edward 'Ned' Kelleher
Lieutenant Patrick Brunton
Adjutant Michael Walker
Quartermaster Chris Murray
Assistant Quartermaster Con Mulligan
Peadar Breslin
Patrick Rigney

Dr Charles McAuley
Andrew McDonnell
Denis 'Dinny' O'Brien
Seoirse Plunkett
Jack Plunkett
James Ryan
Anthony Woods
Eamon Martin
Michael Chadwick
Jimmy Ryan
John Keogh
James Hennessy
Edward Brennan
Shaun Harburn
Robert Briscoe
William Duffy
Frank Kiddie
Robert Burns
Mattie Connolly
George Connolly
William 'Bill' Cregan
Arthur Murphy
Liam Doyle

This list is compiled from the Joe McHenry Collection, Kilmainham Gaol, Military Archives, Ernie O'Malley notebooks (UCD) and pension applications.

ENDNOTES

Chapter 1

1. Arthur Griffith, Michael Collins, Robert Barton, Éamonn Duggan and George Gavan Duffy were the members of the Irish delegation who signed the Treaty.

2. Valiulis, *Portrait of a Revolutionary*, p. 122.

3. Those of the GHQ Staff who rejected the Treaty were Rory O'Connor, director of engineering; Seán Russell, director of munitions; and Seamus O'Donovan, director of chemicals and purchases. The commanding officers of the 1st, 2nd and 3rd Southern Divisions, the 2nd, 3rd and 4th Western Divisions, the 4th Northern Division and the majority of the Dublin Brigade also rejected the Treaty. For more details, see O'Malley, *The Singing Flame*, p. 49.

4. The letter was signed by Liam Lynch, Thomas Maguire, M. McCormack, Andy McDonnell, M. MacGiollarnaid, Liam Mellows, Rory O'Connor, James O'Donoghue, Liam Pilkington and Oscar Traynor.

5. Collins had hoped that the constitution would be Republican enough in its terms to appeal to the anti-Treaty side and thus avoid a split in the army. This was an unrealistic goal, as the British would never agree to a constitution that undermined the Treaty in any way.

6. Paddy O'Daly was a member of Michael Collins' Squad during the War of Independence. After the burning of the Custom House on 25 May 1921, which saw many members of the Active Service Unit arrested, O'Daly became O/C of the 'Dublin Guard'. This was an

amalgamation of the remnants of the Active Service Unit and the Squad.

7.   The term Free State did not come into being until December 1922, so the pro-Treaty side will be referred to as the National Army, National forces, or pro-Treaty forces, unless it has been used in a quotation.

8.   For details on the problems faced by the National Army in the early stages, see Pinkman, *In the Legion of the Vanguard*, pp. 85–95.

9.   For more details on the 'Limerick Crisis', see Ó Ruairc, *The Battle for Limerick City*.

10. There are discrepancies in the records of the actual numbers of those who attended the Convention. Some sources state 211, while others state that between 223 and 228 delegates attended.

11. Valiulis, *Portrait of a Revolutionary*, p. 138.

12. The Belfast Boycott was first introduced on September 1920 in response to the ongoing violence towards Catholics in Belfast. As a result, all goods and services from Belfast were to be boycotted by the rest of the country.

13. Annie Farrington, Bureau of Military History Witness Statement 749.

14. *Ibid.*

15. The positions on the headquarters staff were the same as those on the Executive and were as follows: Liam Lynch, chief-of-staff; Liam Mellows, quartermaster general, Rory O'Connor, director of engineering; Joseph McKelvey, deputy chief-of-staff; Ernie O'Malley, director of organisation, Florrie O'Donoghue, adjutant general, Seán Moylan, director of operations; Frank Barrett, O/C 1st Western Division; Michael Kilroy, O/C Western Command; Liam Deasy, O/C 1st Southern Division; Peadar O'Donnell, Colonel Commandant; P.J. Ruttledge; Seamus Robinson, O/C 3rd Tipperary Brigade; Joseph O'Connor, O/C 3rd Battalion Dublin Brigade; Seán

O'Hegarty, O/C No. 1 Brigade 1st Southern Division; and Tom Hales, O/C 3rd Cork Brigade.

16. O'Malley, *The Singing Flame*, p. 67.

17. Valiulis, *Portrait of a Revolutionary*, pp. 138–139.

Chapter 2

1. The Fowler Memorial Hall, which was in Parnell Square, quite close to No. 44 had been seized by the Republicans on 25 March. The hall, which belonged to the Orange Order, was used to house many refugees from Belfast. Other buildings seized later by the Dublin Brigade were Kilmainham Gaol on 16 April, the Kildare Street Club and the Dublin Port and Docks Offices on 2 May, and Messrs Lever Bros on 3 May.

2. Hopkinson, *Green Against Green*, p. 73.

3. *Irish Independent*, 15 April 1922.

4. O'Malley, *The Singing Flame*, p. 68.

5. *Ibid.*, p. 70.

6. *Ibid.*, p. 71.

Chapter 3

1. Pinkman, *In the Legion of the Vanguard*, pp. 85–86.

2. *Ibid.*, pp. 94–95.

3. Macardle, *The Irish Republic*, p. 702.

4. Neeson, *The Civil War 1922–23*, p. 100.

5. Hopkinson, 'The Civil War from the Pro-Treaty Perspective', *The Irish Sword*, p. 289.

6. O'Malley, *The Singing Flame*, p. 74.

7. The document was signed by Dan Breen, Tom Hales, Humphrey Murphy, Florrie O'Donoghue and Seán O'Hegarty, on behalf of the Republicans. Representing the pro-Treaty side were Seán Boylan,

Michael Collins, Richard Mulcahy, Eoin O'Duffy and Gearóid O'Sullivan. Hales, O'Donoghue and O'Hegarty were initially members of the Executive, but later resigned their positions as a result of differences with the other members.

8.   Those on the committee were Seán Hales (brother of Tom), Seán MacEoin, Joseph McGuinness, Seamus O'Dwyer and Pádraig Ó Maille on the pro-Treaty side. The anti-Treaty representatives were Harry Boland, Kathleen Clarke, Liam Mellows, Seán Moylan and P. J. Ruttledge.

9.   The anti-Treaty members were Liam Lynch, Liam Mellows, Seán Moylan, Rory O'Connor and Seamus Robinson. The pro-Treaty members were Michael Collins, Richard Mulcahy, Diarmuid O'Hegarty, Eoin O'Duffy, Gearóid O'Sullivan and Seán MacEoin.

10. Hopkinson, *Green Against Green: The Irish Civil War*, p. 96.

11. For more details on the pact, see Valiulis, *Portrait of a Revolutionary*, pp. 145–146, 152–153; Hopkinson, *Green Against Green*, pp. 97–100.

12. Murphy, 'The Irish Civil War 1922–23: An Anti-Treaty Perspective', *The Irish Sword,* p. 298.

13. The officers on the anti-Treaty side were Liam Lynch, Rory O'Connor, Ernie O'Malley and Seán Moylan. On the pro-Treaty side were Richard Mulcahy, Eoin O'Duffy, Gearóid O'Sullivan and Seán McMahon.

14. Labour won seventeen seats, Farmers won seven, Independents six, and Trinity College Dublin four.

Chapter 4

1.   Andrews, *Dublin Made Me*, p. 243.

2.   There has been much debate on whether Michael Collins had any involvement in ordering the assassination of Wilson some time previously. There is ample evidence to suggest that he did order the

shooting. Despite efforts to free both men from prison, the British later executed Dunne and O'Sullivan.

3. General Macready was most anxious that the attack should not happen, as it could reunite the IRA. After much deliberation, it was decided to let the Provisional Government handle the situation, and the proposed attack did not materialise.

4. Ferguson's was a Protestant firm, and in the face of the boycott had continued to import cars.

5. O'Malley, *The Singing Flame*, p. 89.

Chapter 5

1. The six were Ernie O'Malley, Joe McKelvey, Rory O'Connor, Peadar O'Donnell, Tom Derrig and Liam Mellows.

2. Three mines had been laid by the garrison when the courts were first taken over. Some of the men involved in the work of laying the mines were John Whelan, Walter Carpenter and Vincent Poole, all members of the Irish Citizen Army who were attached to the 5th Battalion, Dublin Brigade, also known as the Engineers.

3. Donnelly, *The Stand and Fall of the Four Courts*.

4. O'Malley, *The Singing Flame*, pp. 92–93.

5. *Ibid.*, p. 93

6. Younger, *Ireland's Civil War*, pp. 321–322. Two more eighteen-pounder guns were handed over to Dalton later.

7. Macardle, *The Irish Republic*, p. 745.

8. O'Malley, *The Singing Flame*, p. 95.

9. Younger, *Ireland's Civil War*, p. 323.

Chapter 6

1. Younger, *Ireland's Civil War*, p. 324.

2. Pinkman, *In the Legion of the Vanguard*, p. 114. See also Younger, *Ireland's Civil War*, p. 321, for Dalton.

3. Donnelly, *The Stand and Fall of the Four Courts*.

4. O'Malley, *The Singing Flame*, p. 97.

5. For more details, see Deasy, *Brother Against Brother*, pp. 46–51; Valiulis, *Portrait of a Revolutionary*, pp. 155–156.

6. O'Malley, *The Singing Flame*, pp. 98–99.

7. O'Malley notebooks, UCD Archives, P17b/87. There is some discrepancy over Gogan's name. In O'Malley's notebooks, he is referred to as Jim, but there was also in the Red Cross Section a Lieutenant Vincent Gogan and a Steve Gogan.

8. *Ibid.*

9. Donnelly, *The Stand and Fall of the Four Courts*.

10. *Irish Independent*, 29 June 1922.

11. *Ibid.*

12. Dublin Corporation Fire Brigade Department, *60th Annual Report*, p. 30.

13. *Irish Independent*, 9 June 1922.

14. Fox, *The History of the Irish Citizen Army*, p. 218.

15. *Ibid.*

16. Annie Farrington, Bureau of Military History Witness Statement 749.

17. Paddy Kelly, Bureau of Military History Witness Statement 726.

18. Seán Prendergast, Bureau of Military History Witness Statement 802.

19. *Ibid.*

20. Anon., *The Drama of Eight Days* [a pamphlet with no author name], p. 6.

21. *Ibid.*

22. Ward, *In Their Own Voice*, pp. 144–145.

Chapter 7

1.   *Irish Independent,* 30 June 1922.
2.   Ward, *In Their Own Voice,* p. 145.
3.   Younger, *Ireland's Civil War,* p. 326. The British stationed in the Phoenix Park depot were also hit by misguided shells.
4.   Donnelly, *The Stand and Fall of the Four Courts.*
5.   O'Malley, *The Singing Flame,* p. 103.
6.   Pinkman, *In the Legion of the Vanguard,* p. 115. The term Irregulars was a derogatory name to describe the anti-Treaty forces. It will be only used when in a quotation, otherwise the terms for the anti-Treaty forces will be Republicans or anti-Treaty forces.
7.   *Ibid.,* pp. 115–116.
8.   Fox, *The History of the Irish Citizen Army,* p. 219.
9.   *Irish Independent,* 30 June 1922 and CD 288/4, Military Archives.
10. Laurence Nugent, Bureau of Military History Witness Statement 907.
11. The Block consisted of a number of buildings stretching from the Tramway Office on the corner of Cathedral Street up to Findlater Place on the east side of Upper O'Connell Street. The buildings included four hotels: the Gresham, the Granville, the Crown and the Hamman. All the buildings were connected as a result of the Republicans burrowing holes throughout the buildings.
12. *Irish Independent,* 30 June 1922.
13. Seán Prendergast, Bureau of Military History Witness Statement 802.
14. Ward, *In Their Own Voice,* pp. 148–149.
15. Seán Prendergast, Bureau of Military History Witness Statement 802.
16. *Ibid.*
17. *Ibid.*

18. Donnelly, *The Stand and Fall of the Four Courts*.

19. O'Malley notebooks, UCD Archives, P17b/87; O'Malley, *The Singing Flame*, pp. 103–106.

20. Younger, *Ireland's Civil War*, p. 327.

21. Donnelly, *The Stand and Fall of the Four Courts*; O'Malley notebooks, UCD Archives, P17b/98.

Chapter 8

1. O'Malley notebooks, UCD Archives, P17b/87.

2. O'Malley, *The Singing Flame*, p. 110.

3. *Ibid.*

4. *Ibid.*, p. 111.

5. *Irish Independent*, 1 July 1922.

6. O'Malley, *The Singing Flame*, p. 112.

7. Donnelly, *The Stand and Fall of the Four Courts*.

8. Paddy Kelly, Bureau of Military History Witness Statement 726.

9. Fox, *The History of the Irish Citizen Army*, p. 220.

10. *Ibid.*, pp. 221–222.

11. Neeson, *The Civil War 1922–23*, p. 120.

12. *Irish Independent*, 1 July 1922.

13. 'Ireland's Tragic Week', *Irish Life*, 30 June, 7 July and 14 July 1922, p. 17.

14. Ward, *In Their Own Voice*, p. 146.

15. *Ibid.*

16. O'Malley, *No Surrender Here*, p. 31.

17. Donnelly, *The Stand and Fall of the Four Courts*.

18. O'Malley, *The Singing Flame*, pp. 121–122.

19. Younger, *Ireland's Civil War*, p. 331.

20. *Irish Independent*, 1 July 1922.

Chapter 9

1. In most cases the mines that had been laid by the Republicans were viable; however, there were also decoy mines placed on many roads, which created a very tense atmosphere in the city.
2. Seán Prendergast, Bureau of Military History Witness Statement 802.
3. Paddy Kelly, Bureau of Military History Witness Statement 726.
4. Moira Kennedy O'Byrne, Bureau of Military History Witness Statement 1209.
5. Pinkman, *In the Legion of the Vanguard*, p. 117.

Chapter 10

1. *Sunday Independent,* 2 July 1922.
2. *Ibid.*
3. Seán Prendergast, Bureau of Military History Witness Statement 802.
4. MacEoin, *Survivors*, p. 406.
5. Andrews, *Dublin Made Me*, p. 248.
6. Robert Bonfield was later murdered by the pro-Treaty forces, as was John Joe 'J.J.' Stephens, who was a member of the garrison at the Hamman. They were not killed in action but were targeted deliberately and murdered by members of the National Army.
7. Andrews, *Dublin Made Me*, p. 248.
8. Kathleen Barry was the sister of Kevin Barry, executed by the British during the War of Independence. Muriel MacSwiney was the widow of Terence MacSwiney, lord mayor of Cork and commandant of the 1st Cork Brigade, who died on hunger strike in Brixton Prison in October 1920.
9. MacEoin, *Survivors*, p. 407.
10. Pinkman, *In the Legion of the Vanguard*, p. 123.

Chapter 11

1. Seán Prendergast, Bureau of Military History Witness Statement 802.
2. *Ibid.*
3. Ward, *In Their Own Voice*, p. 149.
4. The men were Paul Brady, Martin Finn, Lieutenant Jim Freeney, Captain Jerry Golden, Tom Habesy, Lieutenant P. Kirk, Paddy Mahon, Jimmy McArdle, James McGuinness, Larry O'Connor, Seán Prendergast and Bertie Somerville.
5. Seán Prendergast, Bureau of Military History Witness Statement 802.
6. Younger, *Ireland's Civil War*, p. 335.
7. This armoured car was named after the 2nd Battalion, Dublin Brigade, IRA, who, when the Treaty was signed, predominantly accepted it and had joined the National Army. Their commanding officer during the War of Independence was Tom Ennis, now O/C of the 2nd Eastern Division. Most of these men had been involved in the attack on the Custom House on 25 May 1921 and went on to form the Dublin Guards, the nucleus of the National Army.
8. MacEoin, *Survivors*, p. 408.
9. Pinkman, *In the Legion of the Vanguard*, p. 125.
10. *Ibid.*, p. 125.
11. *Ibid.*, p. 126.
12. O'Malley & Dolan, *No Surrender Here*, p. 48.

Chapter 12

1. *The Irish Times*, 4 July 1922.
2. Pinkman, *In the Legion of the Vanguard*, p. 129.
3. *Ibid.*, p. 130.

4.   *Ibid.*, p. 131.
5.   *The Irish Times*, 4 July 1922.
6.   Ó Duigneáin, *Linda Kearns*, p. 68.
7.   Andrews, *Dublin Made Me*, p. 251.
8.   Annie Farrington, Bureau of Military History Witness Statement 749.
9.   *Ibid.*
10. Dublin Corporation Fire Brigade Department, *60th Annual Report, Year ending 1922*, p. 32.

Chapter 13

1.   *The Irish Times*, 5 July 1922.
2.   Pinkman, *In the Legion of the Vanguard*, p. 134.
3.   *The Irish Times*, 5 July 1922; and 'Ireland's Tragic Week', *Irish Life* (three editions in one), 30 June, 7 July and 14 July 1922, p. 20.
4.   *The Irish Times*, 5 July 1922.

Chapter 14

1.   *The Irish Times*, 6 July 1922.
2.   For more details, see Dublin Corporation Fire Brigade Department, *60th Annual Report, Year ending 1922*, p. 33.
3.   Younger, *Ireland's Civil War*, p. 341.
4.   *The Irish Times*, 6 July 1922.
5.   *Ibid.*
6.   Moira Kennedy O'Byrne, Bureau of Military History Witness Statement 1029.
7.   *The Irish Times*, 7 July 1922.

Chapter 15

1. This gun-carriage had been used in the attack on the Four Courts.
2. *The Irish Times,* 7 July 1922.
3. *Sunday Independent,* 9 July 1922.
4. Bridget O'Mullane, Bureau of Military History Witness Statement 485.
5. Francis Carty, Bureau of Military History Witness Statement 1040; O'Malley, *The Singing Flame,* p. 136.

Chapter 16

1. Hopkinson, *Green Against Green,* p. 122.
2. MacEoin, *Survivors,* pp. 25–26.
3. *Ibid.,* p. 25.
4. Donnelly, *The Stand and Fall of the Four Courts.*
5. Gun History Sheet, PC 625, Military Archives.
6. Donnelly, *The Stand and Fall of the Four Courts.*
7. O'Malley notebooks, UCD Archives, P17b/198.

BIBLIOGRAPHY

Andrews, C. S., *Dublin Made Me* (The Lilliput Press, Dublin 2001)

Anon., *The Drama of Eight Days* (London 1922)

Brennan, Robert, *Allegiance* (Browne and Nolan Ltd, The Richview Press, Dublin 1950)

Briscoe, Robert & Hatch, Alden, *For the Life of Me* (Longmans, Green and Co., London 1959)

Brugha, Maire MacSwiney, *History's Daughter* (O'Brien Press, Dublin 2005)

Deasy, Liam, *Brother Against Brother* (Mercier Press, Cork 1998)

Donnelly, Simon, *The Stand and Fall of the Four Courts* (National Library, MS 33,063)

Dublin Corporation Fire Brigade Department, *60th Annual Report from the Chief of the Dublin Corporation Fire Brigade Department, Year ending 1922* (Dollard, Dublin 1923)

Fox, R. M., *The History of the Irish Citizen Army* (James Duffy and Co. Ltd, Dublin 1944)

Greaves, Desmond C., *Liam Mellowes and the Irish Revolution* (An Ghlór Gafa, Belfast 2004)

Griffith, Kenneth & O'Grady, Timothy E., *Curious Journey: An Oral History of Ireland's Unfinished Revolution* (Hutchinson, London 1982)

Hegarty, Peter, *Peadar O'Donnell* (Mercier Press, Cork 1999)

Hopkinson, Michael, 'The Civil War from the Pro-Treaty Perspective', *The Irish Sword: The Journal of the Military History Society of Ireland*, Winter 1997

Hopkinson, Michael, *Green Against Green: The Irish Civil War* (Gill and Macmillan, Dublin 1998)

Litton, Helen, *The Irish Civil War: An Illustrated History* (Wolfhound Press, Dublin 1995)

Macardle, Dorothy, *The Irish Republic* (Irish Press Ltd, Dublin 1951)

MacEoin, Uinseann, *Survivors* (2nd edn, Argenta Publications, Dublin 1987)

Murphy, Brian P., 'The Irish Civil War 1922–1923: An Anti-Treaty Perspective', *The Irish Sword: The Journal of the Military History Society of Ireland*, Winter 1997

National Graves Association, *The Last Post* (3rd edn, Elo Press, Dublin 1985)

Neeson, Eoin, *The Civil War 1922–23* (Poolbeg Press, Dublin 1995)

Ó Duigneáin, Proinnsíos, *Linda Kearns: A Revolutionary Irish Woman* (Drumlin Publications, Leitrim 2002)

O'Farrell, Padraic, *Who's Who in the Irish War of Independence and Civil War 1916–1923* (The Lilliput Press, Dublin 1997)

O'Malley, Cormac K. H. & Dolan, Anne, *No Surrender Here: The Civil War Papers of Ernie O'Malley 1922–1924* (The Lilliput Press, Dublin 2007)

O'Malley, Ernie, *The Singing Flame* (Anvil Press, Dublin 1992)

Ó Ruairc, Pádraig Óg, *The Battle for Limerick City* (Mercier Press, Cork 2010)

Pinkman, John A., *In the Legion of the Vanguard* (ed. Francis E. Maguire) (Mercier Press, Cork 1998)

Regan, John M., *The Irish Counter Revolution, 1921–1936* (Gill and Macmillan, Dublin 1991)

Robbins, Frank, *Under The Starry Plough: Recollections of the Irish Citizen Army* (Academy Press, Dublin 1977)

Valiulis, Maryann G., *Portrait of a Revolutionary: General Richard Mulcahy and the Founding of the Irish Free State* (Irish Academic Press, Dublin 1992)

Ward, Margaret, *In Their Own Voice* (Attic Press, Cork 2001)

Younger, Calton, *Ireland's Civil War* (Fontana, London 1970)

INDEX

THE BATTLE FOR
LIMERICK CITY

Pádraig Óg Ó Ruairc

ISBN: 978 1 85635 675 6

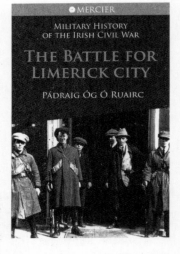

The opening shots of the Irish Civil War in Limerick city were fired on 11 July 1922. The city was of vital strategic importance in the fight for control of the newly independent Ireland, and both Free State and republican troops were determined to secure the city for their respective causes.

At the outset the republicans controlled the city's four military barracks and Thomond and Sarsfield bridges. The Free State forces held the custom house, Limerick prison, the courthouse, William Street RIC barracks and Cruise's Hotel. Battle lines were drawn and over the course of the following two weeks, fighting raged throughout the city until superior numbers and arms gave victory to the Free State army.

Pádraig Óg Ó Ruairc offers a new perspective on the struggle that reduced the viability of the republican's 'Munster Republic' and set the stage for the battle of Kilmallock, which turned the tide of the Civil War in favour of the Free State.

www.mercierpress.ie

Also available from Mercier Press

THE SUMMER CAMPAIGN IN KERRY

Tom Doyle

ISBN: 978 1 85635 676 3

On Wednesday 2 August 1922, Free State troops landed at Fenit pier in the first of a series of seaborne landings on the Cork and Kerry coast. This was a risky and ambitious strategy for the Free State government, whose aim was to surprise the staunchly anti-Treaty republicans in Kerry. By attacking them from an unexpected direction, the government hoped to shorten the war and force the republican forces into a quick capitulation. However, despite the initial success of the landings, the republicans quickly recovered the initiative and over the months of August and September mounted a series of counter-attacks against the Free State army.

Tom Doyle looks at the various successes and failures of both sides in Kerry during the summer campaign of 1922, and how the superior resources of the Free State army and the lack of support from the people for the republicans allowed the Free State to build up a strong presence in a crucial part of the republicans' heartland.